Co

CONNECTICUT BICENTENNIAL SERIES, XIV

Connecticut's Revolutionary Press

By CHARLES L. CUTLER

Globe Pequot

Guilford, Connecticut

Published by Globe Pequot
An imprint of The Rowman & Littlefield Publishing Group, Inc.
4501 Forbes Boulevard, Suite 200, Lanham, Maryland 20706
www.rowman.com

Unit A, Whitacre Mews, 26-34 Stannary Street, London SE11 4AB

Distributed by NATIONAL BOOK NETWORK

Copyright © 1975 by The American Revolution Bicentennial Commission of Connecticut
A Publication of The American Revolution Bicentennial Commission of Connecticut
First Globe Pequot paperback edition 2017

British Library Cataloguing in Publication Information Available

Library of Congress Cataloging-in-Publication Data
The paperback edition of this book was previously cataloged by the Library of Congress as
follows:

ISBN: 87106-063-9
Library of Congress Catalog Card Number: 75-27804

ISBN 978-0-87106-063-1 (paper: alk. paper)
ISBN 978-1-49303-311-9 (electronic)

♾️ᵀᴹ The paper used in this publication meets the minimum requirements of American Nat
Standard for Information Sciences—Permanence of Paper for Printed Library Materials, Al
NISO Z39.48-1992.

Printed in the United States of America

Contents

Illustrations

A sturdy printer, composing stick in hand, sets type.

Foreword

According to John Adams, the American Revolution took place "in the minds and hearts of the people."

Nowhere was this inner struggle more acute than in Connecticut. The eastern and western halves of the state generally disagreed on politics. The east leaned toward the Patriot view; the west showed strong Loyalist tendencies. Throughout the colony, communities dissolved into wrangling factions.

To this day, no one knows what proportion of the people in Connecticut, or America, actually wished to become independent of Great Britain. Some historians feel that a majority never did. But it appears that the number of independence-minded Americans grew during the war.

The shift in public opinion arose from various causes. Some people, even Loyalists, suffered maltreatment from British or Hessian troops. In large areas—including much of Connecticut—social pressure won willing or unwilling converts to the Patriot cause. Certainly, the extraordinary caliber of Revolutionary leaders must have inspired many thousands of the previously indifferent or neutral.

In the forefront of the pressures toward independence stood one that can be readily documented—the Patriot press. Connecticut newspapers, at first impatient with British policies, finally came down bluntly against British rule. Without the newspapers, the marshaling of public opinion against the British government might have come more slowly or not at all.

Editors in Connecticut went well beyond the reporting of public opinion to the molding of it. John Holt, at one time editor of the Connecticut *Gazette*, later bragged to the firebrand Samuel Adams: "It was by means of News papers that we receiv'd & spread the Notice of the tyrannical Designs formed against America, and kindled a Spirit that has been sufficient to repel them."

Connecticut editors like Holt served the cause of the Revolution as effectively as the Minutemen, the veterans of Valley Forge, or the many other heroes of actual combat. Using excerpts from newspapers and other publications wherever possible, this booklet describes the aid of the Connecticut press to the American Revolution. And, since life went on despite the war, here also is a counterpoint of news from Revolutionary Connecticut's home front.

The Stamp Act

F ROM the mid-1760s on, Connecticut's newspapers began to sound more and more Yankee—and less and less British.

The owners of print shops in Hartford, New Haven, New London, and Norwich learned boldness. Radicalized by British taxes, they challenged colonial rule through their newspapers.

With some exaggeration, John Adams said of the Revolutionary generation: "An American who could read and write was as rare as an earthquake or a comet." Yet nonreaders (about six out of seven adults) got the news almost as fast as anyone else. The educated citizens read choice items aloud in homes and taverns, on doorsteps and village greens. Resentment flared up among growing numbers of Americans and found tinder in the repeated miscalculations of British politicians.

Connecticut early became a leader in anti-British journalism. The Connecticut *Courant* (later the Hartford *Courant*) had a circulation that placed it among the largest of the American newspapers. Postriders galloped throughout Connecticut and into Western Massachusetts and New Hampshire with bundles of Connecticut newspapers slung behind their saddles.

From its beginning on October 29, 1764, Hartford's *Courant* had spoken critically about British administration of the American colonies. The first issue complained of the Sugar Act, saying:

> . . . it behooves the colonies to represent their grievances in the strongest point of light, and to unite in such measures as *will be effectual* to obtain redress.
>
> The northern colonists have sense enough, at least the sense of *feeling;* and can tell where the *shoe pinches.*

Complaints like this were not uncommon in the colonies. Yet Parliament, in need of money and insensitive to colonial feelings, debated other kinds of taxes. Prime Minister George Grenville hit on the idea of a stamp tax for America—one that would require the purchase of British stamps for the transaction of business. Such a tax had worked in England. In the spring of 1765, therefore, Parliament overwhelmingly voted a similar Stamp Act for America.

It was a foolish move. Americans were aghast at news that they would be taxed *directly* for the first time. The stamps had to be affixed to legal papers, business documents, college diplomas, dice and playing cards, and publications. Printers had to pay a penny for each four-page copy of their newspapers and two shillings for each advertisement. Since a year's subscription to a weekly colonial paper often cost only six or eight shillings, the Stamp Act threatened some publishers with the loss of about half their newspaper revenue.

Connecticut printer-publishers reacted against the impending tax. That summer, a nephew of Benjamin Franklin, Benjamin Mecom, revived the Connecticut *Gazette* in New Haven, commenting: "Perhaps there never was a more unpromising Time for the Encouragement of another News-paper." But his front page asserted (echoing his distinguished uncle): "Those who would give up *Essential Liberty*, to purchase a little *Temporary Safety*, deserve neither *Liberty* nor *Safety*."

Amid threats of violence, Governor Thomas Fitch issued a warning to Connecticut citizens not to riot. Jared Ingersoll, Stamp Distributor for Connecticut, set out from New Haven for Hartford to learn more about a possible attack against himself. His situation was worse than he thought. On September 23, 1765, the *Courant* blandly described his reception:

> Last Wednesday Afternoon a large Company of able-bodied Men, came to town (on Horseback) from the Eastern Part of this Government, and informed those who were willing to join them, that they were on their Way to New-Haven to demand the Stamp-Officer of this Colony to resign his Office—that a Number of their Companions, were gone on the lower Roads, and that they had all agreed to rendezvous at Branford, the next Day, (Thursday) and that they should tarry in Town that Night; they then dispersed to different Parts of the Town for lodging. . . .

> On Thursday Morning, the whole Body, (including a considerable Number from this Town) set off, on their intended Expedition, and in about an Hour met Mr. Ingersoll, at the Lower End of Wethersfield, and let him know their Business,—he at first refused to comply, but it was insisted upon, that he should resign his Office of Stamp Master, so disagreeable to his Countrymen;—after many Proposals, he delivered the Resignation, mentioned below, which he read himself in the Hearing of the whole Company; he was then desired to pronounce the Words, *Liberty and Property*, three Times, which having done, the whole Body gave three Huzza's; Mr. Ingersoll, then went to a Tavern, and dined with several of the Company:

> After Dinner the Company told Mr. Ingersoll, as he was bound to Hartford, they would escort him there, which they did, to the Number of almost Five Hundred Persons on Horseback. After they arrived in Town, Mr. Ingersoll again read his Resignation in Public, when three Huzza's more were given, and the whole Company immediately dispersed without making the least Disturbance.

The law, nevertheless, went into effect on November 1, 1765. A special edition of the *Courant*, with skull and crossbones at the top, quoted newspapers in New Jersey, New York, Rhode Island, and Massachusetts against the Stamp Act. Then the *Courant* fell silent for five weeks, presumably to avoid the hated tax. The New London *Gazette* and Mecom's Connecticut *Gazette* appeared defiantly without stamps.

In April, 1766, a Hartford broadside—a sheet printed on one side with an official proclamation or special news—claimed that the Stamp Act had been repealed. This report was premature, but the British government had in fact begun to wilt in the face of American opposition. The following month a broadside in New Haven accurately announced the tax's end—"Glorious News. Constitutional LIBERTY Revives!" A personal touch appeared at the bottom of the broadside, where the rider who brought the news from Boston asked for donations at Mr. Beers's Tavern to defray his expenses.

Lacking independent news sources, colonial printers borrowed wholesale from one another. The main text of "Glorious News" had been published simultaneously by the four Boston printers. It came out thereafter in Newport, Rhode Island, and, with some local touches, in New Haven.

Connecticut citizens greeted the repeal with parties and public celebrations. The festivities in Hartford, however, were marred by a disaster recorded in the May 26, 1766, *Courant:*

> The morning was ushered in by the ringing of bells; the shipping in the river displayed their colors; at 12 o'clock 21 cannon were discharged and the greatest preparations making for a general illumination.

> But sudden was the transition from the height of joy to extreme sorrow. A number of young gentlemen were preparing fireworks for the evening in the chamber of the large brick school house, under which a quantity of powder granted by the Assembly for the purposes of the day, was deposited.

> Two companies of militia had just received a pound a man, by the delivery of which a train was scattered from the powder cask to the distance of three rods from the house where a number of boys were collected who, undesignedly and unnoticed, set fire to the scattered powder which soon communicated to that within doors and in an instant reduced the building to a heap of rubbish . . . .

Six men were killed in the explosion and more than 20 people were injured.

Governor Fitch took official note of the repeal with a Proclamation published in New London as a broadside, "For a Day of Fasting and Prayer." Not only were Connecticut citizens to repent of their sins on the designated day, April 16, they were also to pray for the King and "for the better Establishment of LIBERTY and PEACE in our Nation and Land."

The Stamp Act forced printers and others to buy stamps such as this and affix them to various items.

Early Printers

GONE though the Stamp Act was, it left behind injured feelings and a first taste of defiance. The most influential classes of Americans, including printer-publishers, had felt the sting of the tax. They had learned the power of the press. And, almost as important for the future of the country, they had been reminded that they could defy authority and get away with it. The trial of Peter Zenger in 1735 had established, for that New York printer at least, the right to attack royal authority. Now Connecticut printers stood ready, if need be, for battle with Parliament.

The printers of Connecticut were not ordinary people. They showed a passion for the public interest that often went beyond any business advantage that might be gained from their editorial positions. This may have been partly due to Yankee self-reliance. But, for the founders of three of Connecticut's four Revolutionary War newspapers, a long family tradition at least confirmed such a trait. These stalwarts were Timothy Green, founder of the New London *Gazette,* and Thomas Green, founder of both the Hartford *Courant* and the New Haven *Post Boy.*

Members of the Green family had played a prominent role in early Connecticut printing—as they had for a century and a half in New England. Their story began almost at the start of English settlement. Samuel Green, the patriarch, came to America in 1630 at the age of 16. Conditions were so hard for him at first that he had to live in a large cask as his only protection from the weather.

Young Samuel, nevertheless, learned the printing trade and, in time, took over the print shop in Cambridge, Massachusetts—printers for Harvard. He also taught the trade to at least three of his sons. They perpetuated the family's vocation until more than twenty Greens in the following generations had become printers in their turn.

One of Samuel Green's sons, Timothy, moved to New London in 1714 and became the colony's second printer. (The first was the brother of his sister-in-law!) The dynasty of Greens continued to flourish in Connecticut, to the point where it is sometimes hard to distinguish one member from another. *Another* Timothy, grandson of the first, founded the New London *Gazette* in 1763. This newspaper, which succeeded one published for five years in the same town by still another Green, became a leader in raising Connecticut's revolutionary fervor. Little seems known about the editor, other than that he was regarded as "a firm and honest Whig."

Much more is known about the latter Timothy's brother, Thomas Green, founder of two of Connecticut's newspapers that appeared during the Revolution. Young Thomas learned the family trade in New

London, then worked for a firm in New Haven for seven years until a change in management made his position less comfortable. He decided to set up a shop in Hartford—one of the colony's two capitals, yet lacking a printer.

Thomas Green began business October 29, 1764, on Main Street near the North Meeting House and over James Mookler's barber shop. His sign out front showed a heart topped by a crown, above which soared a bird carrying a letter in its beak. The symbolism remains somewhat obscure, but the heart may have been a pun on "Hartford" and the airborne letter an earnest of swift news.

In the same month that Thomas established himself in Hartford, he put out the sample first issue of the Connecticut *Courant*, numbered 00. This promised to include the best news from other newspapers and stated that "great Care will be taken to collect from Time to Time all domestic Occurrences, that are worthy the Notice of the Publick; for which, we shall always be obliged to any of our Correspondents, within whose Knowledge they may happen."

Like other printers of the time, Thomas did not confine himself to the activities considered normal for a modern printer. He also operated a combination book and stationery store. The *Courant* for September 16, 1765, gave a list of his wares:

> To be sold, at the Heart and Crown, Opposite the State-House, in Hartford: Plain and gilt Bibles—Common Prayer Books, plain & gilt—Testaments—Dillworth's Spelling Books—Psalters—Death of Abel, neatly bound and gilt, Ditto, stitch'd—Tryal of Abraham—Watts's Psalms—Tate and Brady's Ditto—Penetential Cries—Royal Primer—Reading, no Preaching—War, an Heroic Poem—Mayhew's Thanksgiving Sermons, Ditto, on Popish Idolitry—Winthrop's Voyage from Boston, to New-foundland, to observe the Transit of Venus, June 1, 1761.—The Rights of the British Colonies—Mather's Dissertations, concerning the venerable Name of Jehovah—New-England's Prospect: Being a true, lively, and experimental Discription, of that Part of America, called New-England, by William Wood.—Small Histories, Plays, &c.—2, 3, 4, and 5 Quire Account-Books, Copy Books, Dutch Quills, and Pens—Slates—Wafers in Boxes—Red and black Sealing-wax—Memorandum Books—Pewter and Led Ink-Stands—Leather Ink-Pots—Temple and common Spectacles, in Cases—Painted Ink-Chests—Holman's genuine Ink-Powder—Horn-Books—Writing-Paper, &c.

Three years after starting the *Courant*, Thomas Green hired young Ebenezer Watson and taught him the printing trade; soon Watson became a partner. Meanwhile, Green began a second newspaper, in New Haven, though he still retained a financial interest in the Hartford shop. The *Courant* informed the public of the new arrangement:

New-Haven, April 16, 1768

The Situation of my Business at Hartford, having made my Return to this Place necessary, I earnestly request of all my Customers there, indebted for News-Papers, and on every other Account, to make immediate Payment, either in Cash, or Country Produce, to Mr. Ebenezer Watson, at the Printing-Office in Hartford, whose Receipt shall be a Discharge, for any payments made to him, on my Account.—And as my Connections in the Printing Business there, in some Measure, still subsist, I hope for the Continuation of the Public Favors.

I take this Opportunity of returning my unfeigned Thanks, for the Kindnesses conferred on me, and my Family, by the Neighborhood, in which we were so happy to reside, while we liv'd in Hartford.

Thomas Green

The Print Shop

T HE newspapers at the command of the printers came forth under primitive conditions. People of that time had little inkling of the modern editor's function. News items and moralistic essays seem often to have been dropped into the newspaper columns as received; major news nearly as often appeared inside the paper as on page one.

The act of printing was laborious, having changed little from Johann Gutenberg's methods of more than two centuries before. Compositors set the text from trays of movable type, then locked the completed page in a frame. Pressmen placed the form in position on the press, inked the type, and laid a sheet of paper over it. One man pulled a lever pressing the paper onto the inked surface. So much strength was required for pulling this lever that the right shoulders and feet of men regularly doing it became enlarged and they tended to walk sideways. The printing process had to be repeated for each page, and the output amounted to about 200 pages an hour. It is hardly surprising that the four-page newspapers of the late colonial era customarily came out only once a week.

Assisting the pressmen were apprentices, youths signed up by the printer for a number of years while they learned the trade. These boys did the dirty work in the shop. They swept floors, lit fires, sorted type, readied ink swabs. "Ads" frequently appeared for such boys, and the turnover must have been high. The following typical advertisement was carried in the Norwich *Packet* for April 20, 1775:

WANTED,

As an apprentice by the Printers hereof, an intelligent young Lad, about 13 or 14 Years of Age, he must read well, write tolerably, be active,

The Connecticut Courant.

MONDAY, OCTOBER 29, 1764.   (Number oo.)

HARTFORD: Printed by T.HOMAS GREEN, at the Heart and Crown, near the North-Meeting-Houfe.

Hartford, October 29th, 1764.

OF all the Arts which have been introduc'd amongft Mankind, for the civilizing Human-Nature, and rendering Life agreeable and happy, none appear of greater Advantage than that of Printing. for hereby the greateft Genius's of all Ages, and Nations, live and fpeak for the Benefit of future Generations.—

Was it not for the Prefs, we fhould be left almoft intirely ignorant of all thofe noble Sentiments which the Antients were endow'd with.

By this Art, Men are brought acquainted with each other, though never fo remote, as to Age or Situation; it lays open to View, the Manners, Genius and Policy of all Nations and Countries and faithfully tranfmits them to Pofterity.—But not to infift upon the Ufefulnefs of this Art in general, which muft be obvious to every One, whofe Thoughts are the leaft extefive.

The Benefit of a Weekly Paper, muft in particular have its Advantages, as it is the Channel which conveys the Hiftory of the prefent Times to every Part of the World.

The Articles of News from the different Papers (which we fhall receive every Saturday, from the neighbouring Provinces) that fhall appear to us, to be moft authentic and interefting fhall always be carefully inferted; and great Care will be taken to collect from Time to Time all domeftic Occurrences, that are worthy the Notice of the Publick; for which, we fhall always be obliged to any of our Correfpondents, within whofe Knowledge they may happen.

The CONNECTICUT COURANT, (a Specimen of which, the Publick are now prefented with) will, on due Encouragement be continued every Monday, beginning on Monday, the 19th of November, next: Which Encouragement we hope to deferve, by a coftant Endeavour to render this Paper ufeful, and entertaining, not only as a Channel for News, but affifting to all Thofe who may have Occafion to make ufe of it as an Advertifer.

☞Subfcriptions for this Paper, will be taken in at the Printing-Office, near the North-Meeting-Houfe, in Hartford.

BOSTON, October 1

IT is now out of fafhion to put on mourning at the funeral of the neareft relation, which will make a faving to this town of twenty thoufand fterling per annum.—It is furprizing how fuddenly, as well as how generally an old cuftom is abolifhed, it fhows however, the good fenfe of the town, for it is certainly prudent to retrench our extravagant expences, while we have fomething left to fubfift ourfelves, rather than be driven to it by fatal neceffity.

We hear that the laudable practice of frugality is now introducing itfelf in all the neighbouring towns, (and it were to be wifhed it might thro'out the government) an inftance of which we have from Charleftown, at a funeral there the beginning of laft week, which the relatives and others attended, without any other mourning than which is prefcribed in a refcent agreement.

October 8. There feems to be a difpofition in many of the inhabitants of this and the neighbouring governments to cloath themfelves with their own manufacture.—At Hampftead, on Long Ifland, in the Province of N. York, a company of gentlemen have fet up a new woolen manufactory, and having given notice to gentlemen fhopkeepers and others, of any of the provinces, that by fending proper patterns of any colour, they may be fupplied with broad-cloths, equal in finenefs, colour, and goodnefs, and cheaper than any imported: the proprietors give good encouragement to any perfon who are any way vefted in the woolen manufactory, fuch as wool combers, weavers, clothiers, fhearers, dyers, fpinners, carders, or underftand any branch of the broad-cloth, blanket, or ftroud manufactory.——At Jamaica on the faid ifland, one Tunis Polpham is erecting a fulling-mill, which will be completat in about a month, and carry on all the branches of a fuller and dyer of cloth.

not be true in fact, that the feverity of the new a—t of p——t is to be imputed to letters, reprefentations, NARRATIVES, &c. tranfmitted to the m——y about two years ago by perfons of eminence this fide the water—And that fome. copies of letters are actually in this town, and others foon expected. —To whatever caufe thefe feverities are owing, it behooves the colonies to reprefent their grievances in the ftrongeft point of light, and to unite in fuch meafures as *will be effectual* to obtain redrefs.

The northern colonifts have fenfe enough, at leaft the fenfe of *feeling*; and can tell where the *fhoe pinches*—The delicate ladies begin to find by experience, that the Shoes made at LYN are *much eafier* than thofe of the make of Mr. Hofs of London—What is become of the noted fhoemaker of *Effex?*

It is fear'd by many who wifh well to *Great Britain*, that the new A—t of P——t will greatly diftrefs, if not totally ruin fome of HER OWN manufactures—It is thought that by means of this A—t, lefs of her woolen cloths, to the amount of fome thoufands fterling, will be purchas'd in this cold climate the infuing winter.

We are told that all the Funerals of laft Week were conducted upon the new Plan of Frugality.

Nothing but FRUGALITY can now fave the *diftrefs'd* northern colonies from impending ruin—It ought to be a confolation to the good people of a certain province, that the greateft man in it exhibits the moft rigid example of this political as well as moral virtue.

A furprizing concatenation of events to one man in one week.

Publifhed a Sunday—married a Monday—had a Child a Tuefday—ftole a horfe a Wednefday—banifhed a Thurfday —died a Fnday—buried a Saturday—all in one Week.

NEWPORT, October 15.

Letters from Jamaica inform us that one of the Men of

The first issue of the Connecticut *Courant* set lofty goals for itself. It also offered some snippy comments about British government policies.

docile, and forget all rural Amusements.—It is expected that his Parents or Guardians will engage to furnish him with Board and Cloathing for one Year, or give a Premium adequate for that Purpose—without these Requisites none need apply.

The loss of "rural Amusements," especially, must have been painful.

Among the other productions of the print shop were pamphlets, broadsides, almanacs, magazines, and books. After the Stamp Act, many of these publications took on a more political tone. Even sermons, often printed up for the general public, shared in the trend. For example, we find a pamphlet published in New London: *A Thanksgiving Sermon upon the Occasion of the Glorious News of the Repeal of the Stamp Act, Preached in New Concord, in Norwich June 26, 1776,* by the Reverend Benjamin Throop.

Later the printed sermons grew more formidable, and the Reverend Samuel Sherwood of Fairfield offered the public in 1774: *A Sermon Containing Scriptural Instruction to Civil Rulers and All Free-Born Subjects. In Which the Principles of Sound Policy and Good Government Are Established and Indicated; and Some Doctrines Advanced and Zealously Propagated by New England Tories are Considered and Refuted.*

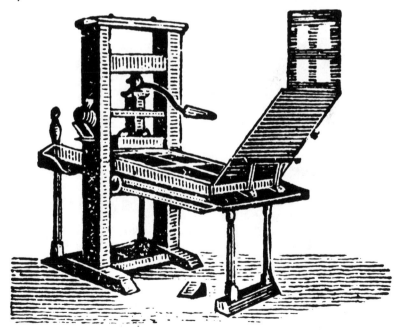

The colonial printing press differed little from Gutenberg's. It was a rugged but cumbersome machine that called for teamwork among its operators.

N EWSPAPERS, too, became more political as the Revolution drew near. But, fortunately for the modern reader, they also furnish glimpses of Connecticut life and thought in other respects. The following letter appeared in the New Haven *Post Boy* for January 25, 1775:

> To the PRINTER,
>
> The Sunday before last as I was going to church, I observed a number of men sawing wood near the Governor's gate; and as I returned from church, several persons were skating on a pond in the common. Surely *these things ought not to be.* I hope in future the civil officers, as well as others, will pay more attention to his Excellency's proclamation *against immortality.*
>
> *Observation.*

Evidence of a looser view can be seen in the New London *Gazette* for April 2, 1773:

> Some time past, as a certain man was crossing Hudson's-River, between New York and Albany, on the ice, having in his hand a bottle of the Good Creature, he fell in, bottle and all, but fortunately got out again; when, missing his bottle, he like a resolute hero, boldly ventured his life, by diving after the same, which he got, and safely took it home to regale his spirits with. A rare instance of courage and love to the juice of the vine. However unaccountable this may appear, it is a fact, and can be proved by several that saw it acted.

The predominating tone, however, was pious, as in the following item from the New Haven *Post Boy* of 1772.

> Plainfield, October 31—Yesterday in the Afternoon came a most violent storm attended with Thunder and Lightning, when one of those pointed Shafts against which there is no resistance, entered the House of Mr. Samuel Cleff, surprisingly shattered it and instantly dried up the Source of Life in the Amiable Partner of his domestic Felicity.
>
> Mrs. Cleff was daughter to Captain Isaac Shepherd, and had been in the Marriage State but about 12 Months. She was an agreeable Companion, and promised much Comfort and Satisfaction to her Friends, especially to the now bereaved Partner of her short Life. She had just arose from a Tea Table, with some others, when the House was struck. One other Person in the Room received a severe Shock, but did not fall, and 'tis supposed the Lightning was attracted by a Curtain Rod, to which Mrs. Cleff stood nearest.
>
> Thus uncertain are earthly Comforts and Enjoyments; when they promise most, they do but disappoint our Expectations, and leave us to regret their Loss in Tears inconsolable.

Broadsides also yield insights into the hopes and fears of the citizens of colonial Connecticut. These printed sheets were intended to be posted or read aloud to groups of people. One with a religious message, printed by Timothy Green in New London in 1768, enthusiastically urged that it be "put into Frames and hung up in Closets, and in every Room in Persons of Qualities Houses, as well as in the Houses of all others of lesser Degree; which the Publisher hereof prays them to consider and put in Practice."

Often broadsides served the same purpose as a modern newspaper extra. Some, in verse, mourned those who died young or in spectacular ways. Thus, Asa Burt of Granville, killed by a falling tree on January 28, 1774, became the subject of a 34-stanza poem published in Hartford. The following excerpt conveys the poem's elevated tone:

IV.

He went into the verdant Wood,
    As Business did him call;
A tow'ring Tree that by him stood,
    He did attempt to fall.

V.

The Tree he cut, and to prevent
    All harm, he backward flee'd,
And lo! a cruel Limb was sent,
    Which light upon his Head!

VI.

No help from Man could he obtain,
    All earthly helps were fled,
Elixir Blood like trickling Rain
    Ran from his wounded Head.

VII.

At length the awful News was heard,
    And help did quickly come:
His weeping friends straitway appear'd
    And brought him to his Home.

VIII.

All Means was us'd for to revive
    To former Health again,
And keep the dying Man alive,
    But Means were all in vain.

IX.

Before the Evening Shades were drew,
    Death stop'd his vital Breath,
His Body fell a Victim to
    The Hands of potent Death.

Glorious News.

Conſtitutional LIBERTY Revives!

NEW-HAVEN, Monday-Morning, May 19, 1766.

Mr. *Jonathan Lowder* brought the following moſt agreeable
Intelligence from *Boſton*.

BOSTON, Friday 11 o'Clock, 16th May, 1766.
THIS Inſtant arrived here the Brig Harriſon, belonging to John Hancock, Eſq; Captain Shubael
Coffin, in 6 Weeks and 2 Days from LONDON, with important News as follows.

From the London Gazette.

Weſtminſter, March 18th, 1766.

THIS day His Majeſty came to the Houſe of Peers, and being in his royal robes ſeated
on the Throne with the uſual ſolemnity, Sir Francis Molineux, Gentleman Uſher o'the
Black Rod, was ſent with a Meſſage from His Majeſty to the Houſe of Commons,
commanding their attendance in the Houſe of Peers. The Commons being come thither accordingly, His Majeſty was pleaſed to give his Royal Aſſent to An ACT to REPEAL an Act made
in the laſt Seſſion of Parliament, intitled an Act for granting and applying certain Stamp-Duties
and other Duties in the Britiſh Colonies and Plantations in America, towards further defraying the
Expences of defending, protecting and ſecuring the ſame, and for amending ſuch parts of the ſeveral Acts of Parliament relating to the trade and revenues of the ſaid Colonies and Plantations,
as direct the Manner of determining and recovering the penalties and forfeitures therein mentioned.

Alſo ten publick bills, and ſeventeen private ones.

Yeſterday there was a meeting of the principal Merchants concerned in the American trade, at
the King's Arms tavern in Cornhill, to conſider of an Addreſs to his Majeſty on the beneficial Repeal of the late Stamp-Act.

Yeſterday morning about eleven o'clock a great number of North-American Merchants went in
their coaches from the King's Arms tavern in Cornhill to the Houſe of Peers, to pay their duty to
his Majeſty, and to expreſs their ſatisfaction at his ſigning the Bill for Repealing the Stamp-Act,
there were upwards of fifty coaches in the proceſſion.

Laſt night the ſaid gentlemen diſpatched an expreſs for Falmouth with fifteen copies of the act,
for repealing the Stamp-Act to be forwarded immediately for New-York.

Orders are given for ſeveral Merchantmen in the river to proceed to ſea immediately on their re-
ſpective voyages to North-America, ſome of whom have been cleared ſince the firſt of November laſt.

Yeſterday meſſengers were diſpatched to Birmingham, Sheffild, Mancheſter, and all the great
manufacturing towns in England, with an account of the final deciſion of ſo auguſt aſſembly relating to the Stamp-Act.

✱✱✱ BOSTON. ✱✱✱

When the King went to the Houſe of Peers to give the Royal Aſſent, there was ſuch a vaſt Con-
courſe of People, huzzaing, clapping Hands, &c. that it was ſeveral Hours before His Majeſty
reached the Houſe.

Immediately on His Majeſty's Signing the Royal Aſſent to the Repeal of the Stamp-Act, the
Merchants trading to America, diſpatched a Veſſel which had been waiting, to put into the firſt
Port on the Continent with the Account.

There were the greateſt Rejoicings poſſible in the City of London, by all Ranks of People, on
the TOTAL Repeal of the Stamp-Act. The Ships in the River diſplayed all their Colours, Il-
luminations and Bonfires in many Parts. In ſhort, the Rejoicings were as great as ever was known
on any Occaſion.

It is ſaid the Acts of Trade relating to America would be taken under Conſideration, and all
Grievances removed. The Friends to America are very powerful, and diſpoſed to aſſiſt us to the
utmoſt of their Ability.

It is impoſſible to expreſs the Joy the Town is now in, on receiving the above great, glorious
and important News. The Bells in all the Churches were immediately ſet a Ringing, and we
hear the Day for a general Rejoicing will be the Beginning of next Week.

Extract of a Letter from New-London, *to* New-Haven, *dated* May 17, 1766.
"I give Joy on the total Repeal of the Stamp-Act. We have the news at New-London Saturday Night 9 o'clock, at 10 the Guns in the Fort are firing on the Joyful occaſion ; Drums beating,
&c. I am now with the Gentlemen of the Town on the Occaſion."

N. B. *Like Rejoicings now* (Monday Morning) *in New-Haven.*

NEW-HAVEN: Printed by *B. Mecom*, for the Entertainment of the People
in general, and his good Cuſtomers in particular.

Mr. Lowder *having rode very hard to bring the above Glorious Tidings, it is not doubted the Sons of
Liberty will be generous in helping to defray his Expences. 'Tis deſired that ſuch Donations be left at Mr.
Beers's Tavern*

—Revolutionary New England, James Truslow Adams

Broadsides carried news that couldn't wait for the weekly newspaper or fit
into it. The basic text above came from a broadside printed in Boston.

From Hartland, Consider Tiffany—storekeeper, farmer, teacher, and an author of local note—furnished another example of these newsy poems. His subject was the death by lightning (evidently worrisome to the colonials) of six young people during June, 1767. One of the four episodes described took place in Hartford's North Meeting House on the 14th of the month. Lightning struck the steeple, ran down the side of the church, and entered the building. Two people were hit, and panic seized the congregation. Here is part of Tiffany's account:

> Their meeting-house was sorely shock'd
> Upon the Sabbath Day,
> While multitudes therein was flock'd
> To hear God's word and pray.
>
> The lightning did the steeple tare,
> And split the same asunder;
> The meeting house was greatly rack'd
> And one was kill'd by thunder.
>
> The hand of God was to be seen
> In that distressing hour,
> For though 'twas crouded full within,
> But one it did devour.
>
> Although that others were struck down
> With this amazing stroke
> The timbers then was hurled down,
> The house being fill'd with smoak.
>
> But let us turn and shed a tear
> On Sarah Larkim's grave,
> Who did submit unto death's spear
> While God the rest did save.

First Clashes

As grievances against Great Britain mounted, Connecticut newspapers devoted more space to political comment and protest. Their radical tendency reflected the election of 1766 as well as the militancy bred by the Stamp Act. The Sons of Liberty had united behind William Pitkin, electing him governor in a political revolution. Thus, radicals were making their presence felt more strongly, both at the grassroots and the official levels.

With one exception, to be noted later, the colony's four newspapers as the Revolution approached, were Whig, or radical, in sentiment. These weekly newspapers did not hesitate to color news or even to indulge in outright propaganda. Such was the case with the Boston Massacre.

The lead article in the *Courant* for March 19, 1770, started with a furious sentence:

B O S T O N, March 12

The town of Boston affords a recent and melancholy Demonstration of the destructive consequences of quartering Troops among Citizens in a Time of Peace, under a Pretence of supporting the Laws and aiding Civil Authority; every considerate and unprejudic'd Person among us was deeply imprest with the Apprehension of these Consequences when it was known that a Number of Regiments were ordered to this Town under such a Pretext, but in Reality to inforce oppressive Measures; to awe and controul the legislative as well as executive Power of the Province, and to quell a Spirit of Liberty, which however it may have been basely oppos'd and even ridicul'd by some, would do Honour to any Age or Country.

The text went on to give a fanciful account of the so-called massacre. British troops supposedly incited peaceful citizens to stage a demonstration, wantonly gunned some of them down on a captain's command, and then wreaked havoc on others trying to rescue the victims. This early atrocity story bore little resemblance to the actual events, and it must have distressed readers who accepted the report at face value.

In the following years, the Connecticut press allied itself steadily more closely with the Whigs and Patriots, finally becoming a mouthpiece for the Revolution. Such partisanship was typical of the American press at that time. It became rare for a newspaper to present objective news or to act as a watchdog against excesses from all quarters. Instead, the editors tended to serve one side or the other with a zeal that seemed to blind them to an alternative viewpoint.

Connecticut citizens trying to uphold the Loyalist side of disputes with the Mother Country early began to find themselves in trouble. Governor Jonathan Trumbull, first elected in 1769 to replace William Pitkin, allowed Patriot groups to exert pressure on both moderates and Tories. One Tory calling himself "Honestus" protested in the New Haven *Post Boy* for January 24, 1772:

Bad as our present Ministers are universally represented to be by the News Papers, they still allow us some degree of Freedom; they suffer us to think, talk, and write as we please, but the Patriots allow us no indulgence: Unless we think, talk, and write as they would have us, we are Traitors to the State, we are infamous Hirelings to the Government.

Soon the British Tea Act of May 10, 1773, was infuriating colonists. In the *Courant* for December 28, 1773, one radical—totally distorting the purpose of the Act—urged Bostonians to resist:

> Parliament an Act has made
> That will distress and ruin trade,
> To raise a tax as we are told,
> That will enslave both young and old;
> Look out poor Boston, make a stand,
> Don't suffer any Tea to land.

In fact, the Boston Tea Party had already taken place by publication time. Connecticut newspapers commented gleefully on that event. Articles in the papers urged local citizens to go and do likewise. Those so inclined found inspiration in a later "Tea Party" reported by the New London *Gazette:*

> LYME, March 17th, 1774
>
> Yesterday one William Lamson, of Martha's-Vineyard, came to this Town with a Bag of TEA, (about 100 Wt.) on Horse-back, which he was pedling about the Country. It appeared that he was about Business which (he supposed) would render him obnoxious to the People, which gave Reason to suspect that he had some of the detestable Tea lately landed at Cape Cod; and upon Examination it appeared to the Satisfaction of all present, to be part of that very Tea; (though he declared that he purchased it of two gentlemen in Newport, one of them 'tis said is a Custom-House Officer, and the other Captain of the Fort,) Whereupon a Number of the Sons of Liberty assembled in the Evening, kindled a Fire and committed the Bag with its contents to the Flames, where it was all consumed and the ashes buried on the Spot, in Testimony of their utter Abhorrence of all Tea subject to a Duty for the Purpose of raising a Revenue in America.
> A laudable Example for our Brethren in Connecticut.

The Brink of Revolution

During 1774, revolutionary rumblings sounded ominously through Connecticut newspapers. Calls for direct action against the British government alternated with pleas to the British Crown. At least several of the printers made their own Patriot views amply known. At the grassroots, incidents such as the following occurred, reported in the *Courant* for July 12, 1774:

We hear from Canaan, that on the 21st of June last, a large number of the most respectable inhabitants of that and the neighboring towns assembled together at the sign of the brazen bull and raised a standard for Liberty, 78 feet high, and fixed a scarlet flag on the top, 15 feet in length, with the words LIBERTY and PROPERTY inscribed on them in large capitals.

As if to offset this militant demonstration, the same issue carried a letter to King George from "AMERICA." The King was respectfully urged to change his nation's policies "before it be quite too late to regain the affections of this country."

The next issue of the *Courant* carried reports of aid from Connecticut to Patriots in Boston after the Port of Boston was closed. A quoted letter from a citizen of Boston to his Hartford friend expressed thanks to the "Free-born Sons of Connecticut" for "sympathetic care and kind Assistance." A vote in Windsor pledged Bostonians "all the assistance in our power, both by our Advice and Counsel as well as giving them part of the Subsistence which God has bless'd us with, from Time to Time as their Necessities shall require."

Political hysteria was also promoted in the July 19, 1774, *Courant*, with a letter from London alleging:

It is a constant practice now with the Ministers here to open all Letters from America that come through the channel of the Post-Office, which are directed to those that they suspect of being Friends to the injured and most oppressed Americans.

Therefore, it is necessary to be cautious what letters are sent by the Packet, or by any Capt. who will not undertake to deliver them as directed with his own hands. . . .

By 1775, with America on the brink of revolution, Connecticut maintained four out of the forty-two newspapers in the American colonies. The following list gives the dates of origin and varying names, simplified in the text, of the Connecticut newspapers existing at this time:

New London *Gazette*—1763 (*The New-London Gazette/The Connecticut Gazette and the Universal Intelligencer*)

Hartford *Courant*—1764 (*The Connecticut Courant/The Connecticut Courant; and the Weekly Advertiser/The Connecticut Courant, and Hartford Weekly Intelligencer/The Connecticut Courant, and the Weekly Intelligencer*)

New Haven *Post Boy*—1767 (*The Connecticut Journal; and New-Haven Post-Boy/The Connecticut Journal*)

Norwich *Packet*—1773 (*The Norwich packet. And the Connecticut, Massachusetts, New-Hampshire, Rhode Island weekly advertiser/The Norwich Packet/The Norwich Packet; and the Weekly Advertiser.*)

Benjamin Franklin's pessimistic nephew had been forced to close his Connecticut *Gazette* in 1768. His last issue included a plea for subscribers to pay up so that he and his family could afford to move out of town.

The majority of the surviving Connecticut newspapers, as in the other colonies, tilted toward the Patriot view of public affairs. Indeed, it was not healthy for them to do otherwise. The following letter in the *Courant,* dealing with a publication by the New York Tory publisher, James Rivington, reflected Whig outrage at the expression of an opposing point of view:

Hartford, November 28, 1774

To The P R I N T E R

Yesterday was published by Mr. James Rivington and sold to many people in town, a pamphlet, with the following false, arrogant, & impudent title, viz.

"Free thoughts on the proceedings of the continental congress held at Philadelphia, Sept. 5, 1774, wherein their errors are exhibited, their reasoning confuted, and the fatal tendency of their non importation, non exportation, and non consumption measures, are laid open to the plainest understanding; and the only means pointed out for preserving our present happy constitution. In a letter to the farmers, and other inhabitants of North-America, in general; and to those of the province of New-York in particular. By a farmer—*hear me, for I will speak."*

The same evening the above pamphlet was read in a company of 20 to 30 inhabitants of this city, who unanimously expressed the utmost abhorrence and detestation of the performance, as being one of the most treacherous, malicious, and wicked productions that has yet appeared, from the implacable enemies of the British colonies and nation.

The author has artfully endeavoured to deceive the ignorant and unwary, and sticks at no falshood to do it; but his reasoning is contemptible, and his conclusions absurd; which will be properly exposed as time will permit—mean while it was with one consent concluded, to treat the pamphlet as it was thought the author deserved to be treated; and it was accordingly committed to the flames.

Since the above, we have just heard that another of the same pamphlets was treated in like manner in another company—And some others burnt before Mr. Rivington's door.   C.D.———

Whigs were torn between a theoretical commitment to freedom of the press and fury at publishers with Tory inclinations. This ambivalence sometimes led the Whigs to argue against themselves. For example, the Committees of Observation (groups set up to carry out the policies of the Continental Congress) for the County of Hartford stated in the Hartford *Courant* of January 30, 1775:

While contending for the liberties of British America in general, we would by no means encourage or countenance any measure that may be construed in any degree to infringe that of the press, on which the others so greatly depend: but on the contrary, conscious of the justice of our cause, and the rectitude of our views, wish to promote to the utmost, freedom of enquiry, and the fair and open discussion of every part of the present most important controversy between Great Britain and her colonies. . . .

Thus far, the Committees would seem to have made a classic case for freedom of the press—one that no civil libertarian could fault. Yet their hearts, it would seem, were not in it. The statement went on to make an exception of the New Yorker, James Rivington:

> Resolved, . . . that it is the opinion of this body, that every sub-scriber in this county, for his paper, called Rivington's Gazetteer, ought forthwith to order him to send them no more, and that no further dealing or correspondence ought to be had with him, unless he satisfy as above [that is, change his ways]:—And they take the liberty to recommend a like conduct towards him, to the other counties in the colony.

Newspaper publishers were shortly given a graphic lesson in what could happen to those with Loyalist views. In April of 1775, a New York enemy of Rivington led some Connecticut Sons of Liberty in a direct assault upon the printer. The mob wrecked his print shop before dispersing. Leading Whigs deplored the incident, but the vandalism must have chilled printers not yet convinced that America should become independent.

The final irony of the Rivington controversy lies in the man's secret activities. Colonel Allison W. Ind states, in *A Short History of Espionage* (McKay, 1963), that Rivington served as a spy for the Patriots. According to this account, the printer's reputation as a Loyalist propagandist gave him access to vital war information—which he relayed to George Washington inside the covers of textbooks.

Printers Under Pressure

T HE mostly Patriot publishers of Connecticut had little to fear personally, and their newspapers grew in circulation under war conditions. Yet the war was a trial for them. Their lives, with the exception of two brothers, reflect and explain the vigorous support of Connecticut newspapers for the Revolution.

Thomas Green by this time had ended his association with the *Courant*. Meanwhile, though, his printing business and newspaper in

New Haven had expanded. His other publications included numerous books, almanacs, and special printed materials for Yale. With his brother, he founded the state's third paper mill in 1776 at a location on the West River just outside New Haven.

The New Haven *Post Boy* survived the turmoil of the Revolution fairly comfortably. Thomas Green had baited the British from the first and had been a leader in opposition to the Stamp Act. Yet, he was an Anglican, and he may have wavered in his loyalties before the war was over. In 1781, President Ezra Stiles of Yale withdrew the college's business from Green, explaining that "The Press in New Haven is a Tory press & unobliging to College. This is the Reason of sending abroad [to Hartford]."

In any case, Thomas continued in business, finally taking his son—also a Thomas—as a partner after his brother Samuel died. A death notice said of the father: "He was a gentleman of peculiar suavity of manner, great benevolence, and universally esteemed; every house in New Haven was to him as a home."

Perhaps Thomas Green's greatest accomplishment, however, was the newspaper he abandoned in its infancy—the Connecticut *Courant*. Under the able leadership of Ebenezer Watson, this quickly began rising to a dominant position among the colony's papers and—as already documented—became a clarion voice for independence.

In 1775, Watson built a paper mill on the Hockanum River in what is now Manchester. Only two years after completion of his mill, Watson died of smallpox. His widow mourned in the *Courant* for September 22, 1777:

> On Tuesday last departed this life after a distressing sickness, Mr. Ebenezer Watson, Printer, in the 34th year of his age. A gentleman of a most humane heart, and susceptible of the tenderest feelings for distress, in whatever manner discovered—Jealous of the rights of human nature, and anxious for the safety of his country, his press hath been devoted to the vindication of rational liberty.
>
> The Governor's company of Cadets, of which he was an Ensign, in token of respect for the deceased, attended the funeral in their uniforms. He has left a melancholy widow, with five young children, and a numerous circle of friends to lament his death.

Watson's widow, the former Hannah Bunce of Lebanon, proved equal to the crisis and began operating her late husband's print shop on her own. Her case was not unique. Beginning with Mrs. Elizabeth Timothy of the South Carolina *Gazette* in 1739, at least eleven women had served as American newspaper publishers before her. All of these women were also the widows of newspaper proprietors.

At the beginning of the new year, Mrs. Watson took on as a partner 20-year-old George Goodwin, who had started with the *Courant* at the age of nine as an errand boy. His entire career with the *Courant*

—*The Hartford Courant*
Hannah Bunce Watson took over the *Courant* in 1777 after her husband's death. She raised the newspaper's circulation and rebuilt its paper mill.

would span 75 years! Within a month of the new partnership, however, the newspaper faced a disaster. Its paper mill burned down, and the partnership of Watson and Goodwin had to apply to the Connecticut legislature for help, with the successful results noted elsewhere in this booklet.

On February 11, 1779, Hannah Watson married a 37-year-old widower next door, Barzillai Hudson. Mr. Hudson, who had followed the trade of mason, also had served as commandant of the county jail at Hartford—a place where war prisoners were kept during the Revolution. The following month, the new husband became a partner in the firm, which was now called Hudson & Goodwin. This new firm sustained the *Courant*, soon acquired an interest in a second paper mill, and, even before the end of the Revolution, published such notable books as the poem *M'Fingal* by John Trumbull and the much-reissued speller by Noah Webster.

Turning from the Greens and their successors, one finds less stability in the early management of Connecticut's fourth Revolutionary newspaper, begun in 1773 under the grandiose name of the *Norwich Packet and the Connecticut, Massachusetts, New Hampshire, & Rhode Island Weekly Advertiser*. This paper was established by the brothers James and Alexander Robertson from New York, with John Trumbull (*not* the author of *M'Fingal*) of Norwich. The Robertsons, natives of Scotland, had early operated newspapers in New York City and in Albany, New York. Trumbull, born in Massachusetts, was not closely related to the famous Connecticut Trumbulls.

The Robertsons sold out their interest in the Norwich *Packet* in May, 1776, to Trumbull. By way of explanation, they declared that "they could no longer carry it on without making it subservient to the Cause of Rebellion." They moved on to Albany and then to New York City. In a few months, they established the *Royal American Gazette* in the city—conclusive proof of the direction of their loyalties, if any had been needed.

James Robertson went to Philadelphia in February, 1778, after the British had secured control of that city. The next month, he began bringing out the *Royal Pennsylvania Gazette*, a semi-weekly that lasted only 25 issues. After a return to New York upon the British evacuation of Philadelphia, James Robertson went to Charleston, South Carolina, and started there a newspaper with the by now unsurprising name of the *Royal South Carolina Gazette*. This lasted more than two years.

With the final defeat of the British, the Robertson brothers moved to Shelbourne, Nova Scotia. There, indomitable to the last, they resumed publication of their old *Royal American Gazette*, picking up the volume and series numbers from where they had left off in New York. Alexander died in 1784, and James eventually returned to his native

27

Edinburgh and continued working there as a printer. For dedication to a cause, it would be hard to find the equal of the Robertson brothers either among Loyalists or Patriots.

As for the John Trumbull who had been left in control of the Norwich *Packet*, he brought the newspaper in line with prevailing opinion and served as editor until his death in 1802.

Press Campaign Against the British

To return to the newspapers as they incited Connecticut citizens against British rule, their campaign continued and became even more pointed. On January 9, 1775, the *Courant* presented a political statement in the form of a supposed soliloquy by Lord North, the British Prime Minister:

> If those stubborn people cannot be cajoled, they must be forced— we must compel them to submit—more soldiers must be sent—But how shall we prevent the desertion of them?—We must send the third regiment of guards—they are a tried corps—we may surely depend upon them.—It will cost a great sum to send forces over sufficient to subdue the obstinacy of those rebellious Americans,—the people of England will grumble to pay new taxes for such a purpose. . . .

Yet just two weeks later, the *Courant* quoted disapprovingly an item from Rivington's New York *Gazetteer* claiming that the government in Hartford had ordered 300 barrels of gunpowder and lead. Rivington asserted that this action showed "a spirit of Independence," but the *Courant's* editor denied such an inference:

> An ardent thirst for liberty, and a noble uniformity of sentiment reigns indeed among all ranks of people, and if occasion should require, we shall doubtless be ready to vindicate our rights at the risk of our lives; but no one even dreams of a state of independence. . . .

The columns of Connecticut newspapers, nevertheless, showed much belligerency. Anti-British news and comments became routine. In the *Courant* for April 3, 1775, a provocative letter said to be from a British soldier stationed in Boston, disparaged Patriots as "destitute of every principle of religion or common honesty." The letter-writer also confidently opined: "As to what you hear of their taking up arms to resist the force of England, it is mere bullying, and will go no farther than words. . . ."

In fact, advertisements appearing in the Connecticut papers offered guns, gun powder, even bayonets. An item in the New Haven

Post Boy for February 2, 1775, sardonically noted the high price of gun powder in Newport because the people there had "bought up almost all there was, to defend themselves against *wolves* and other *beasts of prey.*"

The publishers did not content themselves merely with barbs against British policy. They assailed the Tories in the colony as wrongheaded people not really entitled to express their views. One report in the New Haven *Post Boy* for February 22, 1775, described the reception by Wethersfield Patriots of two Tories from Ridgefield (a town then under Tory control):

WETHERSFIELD, Feb. 14th, 1775

This Evening, two of the Inhabitants of a Place, *lately known, and called, by the Name of Ridgfield,* put up at a public House in this Town, and entering into Conversation, boldly justified the vote, of said *late Town of Ridgfield,* in disapproving of the Doings of the Continental Congress; and proceeded far in supporting Court Doctrines of Passive-obedience to Parliament, &c., which being taken Notice of, by a Number of Gentlemen present, they considered it, in effect, as a direct Breach of the Association of said Congress and thereupon voted, That in their Opinion, it was proper that these Persons should be returned, the Way from whence they came, under safe Conduct, from Town to Town, *to the said Place, lately known, by the said Name of Ridgfield. . . .*

—and the unhappy Men, properly escorted, set off, at nine o'Clock, amid the Hisses, Groans &c. of a respectable Concourse of People,— the Populace following them out of Town, beating a dead March, &c. Not the least Violence was offered, but the whole was conducted with the utmost Regularity—and the Company dispersed, fully resolved, That as no One, of those Principals, is supposed now to be an Inhabitant of this Town, it shall be their Care and Attention, that no such, shall be, hereafter tolerated, within it, no not for a Night.

It is intriguing to note how often harassment of the political opposition was allegedly carried out with the "utmost Regularity"—as above—or without the "least disturbance"—as in the case of Jared Ingersoll, cited earlier. Whigs wished to legitimize their cause and maintain a theoretical support of free speech.

With spring, came the event that carried Patriots beyond vows and demonstrations. The clash on April 19 at Lexington and Concord rallied not only such people, already numerous in Connecticut, but many fence-sitters as well.

At 10 o'clock on that fateful Wednesday morning, the postrider, 23-year-old Israel Bissell, left Watertown, Massachusetts, with details of the crisis. A note from the Massachusetts Committee of Safety ordered: "The bearer Israel Bissell is charged to alarm the country quite to Connecticut and all persons are desired to furnish him with fresh horses as they may be needed."

It ordinarily took postriders about a week to travel the distance from Boston to New York, but the young man set out pellmell on his journey. He reached Worcester, where his hard-ridden horse dropped dead, in only two hours. Then came an overnight wait while the local Committee of Correspondence assembled, copied his message, and fitted him out for the next lap.

At Pomfret, and then Brooklyn, Connecticut, Bissell spread the news. Colonel Israel Putnam, living in retirement in Brooklyn, left his oxen yoked in the field to ride forthwith to Boston and assume command of the Connecticut militia. "Old Put" effectively spread the alarm along his own route.

As Bissell continued southward, through New London and along the shoreline, he cried out the news to citizens. But the mechanics of news dissemination in that era slowed his progress. Committees receiving the written news had to copy it out laboriously. Sometimes they appended their own hasty comments to the original, such as: "For God's sake send this man on without the least delay!" or "Night and day to be forwarded."

Yet the Battle of Lexington was already three days old by the time the announcement of it rang out in New Haven on Saturday morning, April 22—Bissell having arrived the night before. Captain Benedict Arnold called out his troops, the Second Company of Governor's Foot Guards, on the Green and got an enthusiastic response to his proposal for a march to Boston. He then obtained gunpowder from a reluctant Town Committee by drilling the Guards in a menacing manner.

Printers pushed just as hard as Bissell to reduce the serious time lag in the delivery of news. Bissell had traveled in a wide arc around Hartford, so his intelligence reached the editor of the *Courant* relatively late. Nevertheless, Ebenezer Watson managed to include an item about the clash in the April 24 issue, noting "a universal muster of troops in Connecticut."

On May 1, Watson editorialized about Lexington and Concord in a broadside entitled "The *American CRISIS: Let God, and the World judge between Us*." This publication complained about "the late inhuman Murder & Massacre, by a Brigade of near 1,000 savage Soldiers, on a handful of inoffensive Men." It informed readers that the event was an "instance of Rage and Barbarity, unparalleled by the most savage Nation on Earth."

For more than a month, Connecticut newspapers featured reports filtering back from Boston about the battle. On May 8, the *Courant* picked up a five-day-old account from Worcester. This began with the exhortation: "AMERICANS! forever bear in mind the BATTLE of Lexington!" It consisted of atrocity stories, plus a list of American casualties. On May 24, the New Haven *Post Boy* carried on its front page affidavits from a number of Americans claiming that the British had started the fighting.

The accounts of Lexington and Concord appearing in the Connecticut newspapers were partisan, highly colored, and often fanciful. For the Patriot editors (as well as that master propagandist in Boston, Samuel Adams) the event was a godsend. At last the revolutionaries had a decisive issue around which to rally. Whatever had led up to the clash, British troops undeniably had fought a battle with the Americans. The editors worked and reworked this theme, portraying the British soldier as a bloodthirsty monster.

Bissell's ride, and the need for it, pointed up the difficulty of news reports throughout the entire war. News came variously through letters, interviews, oral accounts, and other newspapers or broadsides. Professional reporters had not even been imagined. And travel could be agonizingly slow, with the average voyage from England to America taking seven weeks.

The way was thus open for distortions of important events. Even had editors intended to print objective news about the war, and they usually did not, "hard news" was very hard to obtain. As it was, the editors could give free rein to their imaginations and their passions.

Harassment of the Tories

Wĩᴛʜ the outbreak of hostilities, things got less pleasant in Connecticut for Tory-Loyalists. Committees of Correspondence showed redoubled vigilance in exposing those with the wrong political outlook. Commonly the culprits could escape ostracism only by making a public statement that their views had changed. Such recantations began appearing regularly in Connecticut newspapers. The following from the New Haven *Post Boy* for June 7, 1775, revealed the kind of spirited criticism that the Patriots were eager to suppress:

> I ABRAHAM HICKOX, . . . confess I have not only treated the Continental Congress with disrespect and abuse, but have also greatly abused the General Assembly of this Colony, in saying that they spent their money for nothing, which appears by evidence, tho' I don't myself recollect it, & have also tryed to ridicule the Soldiers which have been raised for the defence of this Colony, by asking the question, whether they intended to fight Gage with their feathers? and at the same time told them that they would go to fight New-England Rum more than anything else; and that the Soldiers enlisted for no other motive but to get the Government's money and to live a lazy life:

Newsboy hands a housewife the paper over a Dutch door. This rare portrayal appeared in a broadside from *The New-York Weekly Museum,* in 1790.

I further have said that the full character of a Whig is a liar, or words to that effect, and that Gage is an honest man, with many other reflections upon the characters and doings of those who in this day of distress, stand forth for the defence of the liberties of this Country.

My conduct herein I acknowledge to be imprudent & unjustifiable, and for which I am sincerely sorry and I do promise for the future, so far as I am able, to behave myself in such a manner as to give no offence to the Community.

Dated New-Haven May 31st 1775.
ABRAHAM HICKOX

Sometimes the punishment meted out to dissenters was left to the reader's imagination, as in the following item from the *Courant* for June 19, 1775:

Capt. Edward Mott's company, being insulted by a couple of rascally *tories,* as they passed through the town of Litchfield, the two offenders found it necessary to extinguish the flames of resentment they had kindled, by eating a hearty meal of what is vulgarly called *Humble Pye.*

Certain actions also brought down vengeance upon the heads of offenders. Tea was proscribed because of its long association with the Intolerable Acts, which had followed the Boston Tea Party. From Farmington, Seth Bird defensively claimed in the columns of the *Courant* (April 24, 1775) that he had expressed a willingness one morning to have a cup of tea only because of a cold caught riding in the wet the night before. John Ransom of Kent made a formal confession in the New Haven *Post Boy* for June 28, 1775, of "once inadvertently using that detestable and obnoxious Vegetable, called East-Indian tea." He asked the public's forgiveness and promised not to err again.

Ebenezer Watson of the *Courant* showed unusual zeal in exposing Loyalists. He freely referred to them as "a Lousey Pack," "Vultures," and "Vermin." For some months, he published in the first column of page one the names of those denounced by Committees of Inspection. These names were to remain until purged by confession. Yet Watson did not want to make this too easy, and on October 16, 1775, he inserted the following notice:

> ∴ *Silvanus Griswold's* second vindication of his conduct for labouring on the late Continental Fast, cannot find a place in this paper till he has first obtained *Liberty* for that purpose, of the Committee of Inspection of the town of *Windsor*.

War Propaganda

Wɪᴛʜ hostilities under way, Connecticut newspapers offered their readers heavy doses of war news and propaganda—atrocity reports, news of American successes on the battlefield, and exhortations to fight. The June 19, 1775, issue of the *Courant* carried a letter from a member of the Continental Congress to the effect that he and other delegates had just voted 70,000 men and three million dollars "for the Common Defence of the Just Rights and Liberties of the American Colonies."

A letter to the editor, signed "America," in the next issue, however, struck a note of desperation:

> A fleet of pirates, and an army of British rebels and murderers are employed to rob us of our property, ravage our country, shed the blood of its innocent inhabitants, and destroy and lay waste our late peaceful dwellings with fire and sword.—The garments of great numbers of our countrymen have already been roll'd in blood. . . . We are drove to the last resort.

Negative news from Great Britain occupied a prominent place in the Connecticut newspapers. Often this indicated British sympathy with the Americans, lack of will to fight, or dissension on the home front. The following comment in the *Courant* for July 10, 1775, cut deeper than most such items, with an attack on the institution of monarchy itself:

A Correspondent observes, that from the present Procedures of several European Princes, it should seem that the Amusement of a King consists in making the World unhappy. The Spanish Monarch has declared War against the Algerines; the Emperor of Morocco, also, avows himself the Enemy of the Dey of Algiers; the King of Prussia is diligently augmenting his Forces, as if meditating some signal Blow; the King of France is preparing a formidable Fleet; and the King of Great Britain is at the Eve of a War with his own Subjects.

Despite the anti-British propaganda and actual bloodshed, many American Patriots still could not swallow complete separation from the mother country. Most had grown up thinking of Great Britain as a distant but worthy parent. Even after Lexington and Concord, a significant number of Americans expected that the political differences with Britain could be settled without drastic measures. A turning point for some of these moderates came with the pamphlet *Common Sense* by Thomas Paine.

Writing from Pennsylvania, Paine called for outright independence from Great Britain. He attacked the idea of hereditary monarchy, and he denied the usefulness of reconciliation with the British. In his introduction, he asserted that the dispute had international import: "The cause of America is in a great measure the cause of all mankind."

Paine claimed a sale for *Common Sense* of 120,000 copies in the three months following its publication in January, 1776. Newspapers throughout the Colonies, including at least three of the Connecticut papers, printed extracts from it, and the *Courant* devoted most of four issues, starting February 19, 1776, to reprinting the complete text. Watson gave two reasons for this extraordinary step—the difficulty in obtaining suitable paper for a pamphlet, and his wish to offer readers promptly "every thing curious, entertaining and instructive."

Paine's words evidently went out to a receptive audience. In June, the Connecticut legislature instructed its delegates to Congress to vote for independence, and Connecticut by then had summoned more than 7,000 men to military service. The Declaration of Independence found Connecticut already imbued with a new spirit. Within weeks of the Declaration, the *Courant* observed that a minister in East Windsor had baptized a baby (sex unspecified) with the name of "Independence." The New London *Gazette* for July 5, 1776, gave the following patriotic marriage notice:

MARRIED. In Mansfield, Mr. Luke Flint, of Windham, to Miss Mary Slate, Daughter of Mr. Ezekiel Slate, an agreeable and happy Pair.— What deserves the public Notice, and may serve to encourage the Manufacturer of this Country, is, that the Entertainment, tho' served up, with good Wine, and other spirituous Liquors, was the Production of their own Fields and Fruit Gardens, assisted alone by a neighbouring Grove of spontaneous Maples.—The Bride and two of her train appeared in genteel Silk Gowns, and others of the Family in handsome Apparel, with sundry Silk Handkerchiefs, etc. intirely of their own Manufacture.

Lingering Servitude

O NE of the profound ironies of the Revolution was the lack of freedom many Americans continued to suffer. For countless people, independence was to mean hardly any change at all in their servitude. The war actually swelled the number already in some form of bondage, as deserters, prisoners of war, and others caught up in social disruption lost their freedom. Connecticut newspapers bore ample testimony to the plight of less privileged people in the community.

Black slaves in Connecticut (about 5,000 of them) were the most obvious of these unfortunate people, both before and during the war. Advertisements for runaways frequently appeared in the columns of newspapers, sometimes in the form of vignettes, such as this from the *Courant* for May 15, 1775:

> Run away from the subscriber on the 23rd inst. a negro man named Prince, about 25 years old, near 5 feet 10 inches high, well set, had with him a red great coat and a violin, on which he plays well, has a small scar on his forehead, and speaks good English. Whoever will take up said negro and return him to his master, shall have a handsome reward and all necessary charges paid, by Elisha Jones.

Slaves were sold through the newspapers or even offered for nothing, as the following astounding notice in the *Courant* for September 18, 1775, indicated:

> To be given away, a very likely, healthy female Negro child of a good breed, is about five months old, any person inclining to take it, may be further informed by applying to the Printer.

The times were not bad for all slaves, however. A few men won their freedom by enlisting with the Patriot forces. Still others seemed to have enjoyed better-than-average opportunities. Jupiter Hammon

Samuel Saurs Calender.

This woodcut is the earliest known picture of a printing press printed in America. Mercury delivers the copy.

appeared in a Hartford broadside on August 4, 1778, as the author of a poem dedicated to the famed black poet of Boston, Phillis Wheatley. Although owned by Joseph Lloyd, Hammon was able to publish his poem, the broadside stated, with the aid of "a number of his friends." His pious address to Miss Wheatley included several stanzas about her arrival in America:

4.

God's tender mercy brought thee here,
Tost o'er the raging main;
In Christian faith thou hast a share,
Worth all the gold of Spain.

5.

While thousands tossed by the sea,
And others settled down,
God's tender mercy set thee free,
From dangers still unknown.

6.

That thou a pattern still might be,
To youth of Boston town,
The blessed Jesus set thee free,
From every sinful wound.

Sometimes apprentices, too, tried to escape their servitude. Typically, these youths were boys. The New London *Gazette*, however, for July 14, 1779, carried an "ad" placed by Samuel Fox, Jr., of that city for a runaway apprentice girl named Lydia Preston, "about 14 years old, born in this town." It is noteworthy that Mr. Fox offered only sixpence for her return and wasn't even sure of the girl's age.

Frequently, relatives received no better treatment than slaves or apprentices. The following curious advertisement appeared in the *Courant* for April 24, 1775:

Runaway from the subscriber a servant man named David Canada, about 20 years of age, light complexion, light coloured hair, slender built, goes stooping forward; had on when he went away a red brown coat, black jacket, deer-skin breeches, blue stockings, calf-skin shoes, pewter shoe buckles, check'd or strip'd woolen shirt; was in company with a tall slim fellow, six feet high. Whoever shall take up said David and return him to his father in Windham shall have 3s. reward and all necessary charges paid by me   DAVID CANADA.
Windham, April 17, 1775.

One can only speculate on the relationship between a 20-year-old son and a father who would advertise for him in such terms.

Some men treated their wives almost as chattels, a circumstance that appeared in advertisements. Typically, the husband notified the world that his wife had deserted him and that no one should either harbor her or give her help. In the following "ad" from the *Courant,* James Maher had the effrontery to denounce his wife and advertise his business at the same time:

> Whereas Esther, the wife of the subscriber, has for some time past behaved in a very unbecoming manner; and I am apprehensive she will do all in her power to injure me—this is therefore to forbid all persons crediting her on my account, as I mean to break off all connection with her, and pay no debt contracted by her after this date.
>
> Hartford, June 27, 1776   James Maher
>
> N.B. Said Maher carries on the set-work [a kind of boat-building] business in its various branches, in the strongest and most genteel manner, at his shop near the water side.

This episode had an unusual twist. Late in the following month, Maher created a disturbance in the Hartford home of a Mrs. Knox and had to be ousted by several officers. The *Courant* described the brawl with a gusto that anticipated crime reporting of a later era:

> Maher in the first place, as an item of his feelings on this occasion consigns Capt. Hill over to damnation and then gives him to understand that if he would venture down he might receive a further conviction of his folly in being so officious in the quarrel, upon which Capt. Hill [descended, and Maher] was soon stretched in an horizontal posture and levelled with the dust. By this time it is easy to see that nothing short of blood could appease the wrath of the incensed Maher. —He arose from the earth and went deliberately to a house at a few rods distance, and having armed himself with a cooper's knife (handle and blade perhaps two feet in length) returned doubtless with intent to take the life of his antagonist, but Capt. Hill defended himself with a billet of wood, till at length he sprang behind him and clinched hold of his arms, whilst Maj. French and [Lieut.] McDermont were endeavoring to wrest the knife from his hands. In this struggle, Maher gave the wound [to McDermont], which probably would have been fatal if the use of his arms, like a man pinion'd, had not been greatly restrained by Capt. Hill. The above is a true representation of the facts, as they appeared from the evidences, on examination before a magistrate.

Apparently chastened by this experience, Maher printed a retraction in the *Courant* for August 5, 1776, of the advertisement against his wife. In tones of alcoholic self-abasement, he stated that he was now aware of his "folly and wickedness." He pledged himself to treat his wife "with tenderness and respect, and to exert myself on all occasions to the utmost of my abilities to render her life comfortable, and to behave in all respects as becomes a kind and tender husband." But such a turnabout, needless to say, was rare.

The state of Connecticut at this time was working hard to recruit soldiers for the Continental Army. On November 6, 1776, a broadside proclamation by Governor Jonathan Trumbull promised Connecticut men who volunteered for the duration of the war, and for at least three years, a bounty in addition to their regular recompense. They were to get "one good blanket" a year, plus the best terms for the provisions and clothing they had to buy. This and other offers apparently were successful, and, for its size, Connecticut stood among the leading states in manpower recruited.

Yet Connecticut servicemen deserted by the thousands before the war's end. By 1777, notices for deserters appeared abundantly in the state's newspapers. The reward for their apprehension was usually $5 or $8 apiece. In the light of debate over amnesty following the Vietnam war, an offer to deserters by George Washington acquires new interest. The following notice appeared prominently on the front page of the New Haven *Post Boy* for April 16, 1777:

> By his Excellency George Washington, Esq.; General and Commander in Chief of the Forces of the United States of America
>
> ### PROCLAMATION.
>
> Whereas many soldiers lately inlisted in the Continental Army, not content with the generous bounties and encouragements granted to them by Congress, but, too much influenced by a base regard to their interest, have reinlisted with, received bounties from, other officers, and then deserted. . . . I have thought proper to issue this my proclamation, offering free pardon to all those above described, as well as to those who have deserted from other motives, who shall voluntarily surrender themselves to any officer in the Continental Army, or join their respective corps before the 15th day of May next. And I do strictly enjoin all officers in the army under my command, and intreat the good people of these States, to use their utmost endeavours to apprehend and secure such deserters as shall not avail themselves of the indulgence offered by this Proclamation.
>
> Given under my Hand at Head-Quarters, Morris-Town, this sixth day of April, 1777.
>
> GEO. WASHINGTON.

On September 2 of the same year, the *Post Boy* felt constrained to publish a defence of New England honor by General Benedict Arnold. A letter from him—ironic in the light of his subsequent behavior—noted charges that New Englanders had failed to enlist in the Army so that the British would occupy New York State, which then could be conquered by and divided up among the New England states. Arnold protested:

> This report so highly reflecting on the New-England States (ever noted for their love of justice, and hospitality of their neighbours) is so very scandalous and ridiculous, that I am convinced that no man of

common sense, who is acquainted with New-England, will give the least credit to it, but look upon it as the last feeble effort of our internal enemies, to divide and distract us.

Meanwhile, because of its relatively sheltered location, Connecticut became a repository for pro-British prisoners. A son of Benjamin Franklin, former Governor William Franklin of New Jersey, lived in several Connecticut towns as a prisoner. Such people inspired disgust in the Patriots, and Ebenezer Watson recorded in the *Courant* for August 5, 1776, the arrival in Hartford of "a motley mess" of 20 or 30 Tories, apparently destined for confinement in New London.

Hard Economics

T HE war years, despite their disruption of Connecticut traditions, were a period of growth for the newspapers in the state. The British occupation of New York shut off Patriot newspapers there, thus increasing the demand for the almost unmolested Connecticut papers. Seventeen of the 42 colonial papers at the beginning of the war did not survive until the war's end; all four in Connecticut lasted past the year 1800.

A major reason for the staying power of the Connecticut press was the advanced technology available in the state. In 1768, Abel Buell of Killingworth began developing the first American-made type. The following year, he petitioned the Connecticut Assembly—in words printed from his own type—for help in setting up a foundry.

The committee examining Buell's plea reported that "he hath Discovered the Art of Letter Founding; & that he is capable of makeing Instruments necessary for the proper Apparatus of Letter Founding. . . ." It recommended that he be granted a loan of £100 on condition that he stay in Connecticut for seven years. It also recommended that he receive a second loan of £100 at the end of the year if he made good progress. Yet Buell, a man of much talent and little stability, did not get around to furnishing Connecticut printers with his type until more than a decade later.

Connecticut also pioneered in the construction of printing presses, producing at least one of the first in America. The *Massachusetts Gazette* for September 7, 1769, reported that:

Mr. Isaac Doolittle, Clock & Watch-Maker, of New Haven, has lately compleated a Mahogany Printing-Press of the most approved Construc-

TO THE HONORABLE THE GENERAL ASSEMBLY OF THE COLONY OF CONNECTICUT, Convened at New-Haven the Second Thursday of October AD 1769:

The Memorial of ABEL BUELL of Killingworth Humbly sheweth;

That your Memorialist having Experienc'd the Great Goodness of this Honorable Assembly, for which he Begs Leave to render his most Grateful Tribute of thanks, and to Assure them from a Grateful Sense of their Clemency he has made it his unwearied Study to render himself Useful to the Community in which he lives and the American Colonies in general, and by his Unwearied application for a number of months past has Discover'd the Art of Letter-Founding; And as a Specimen of his abilities Presents this Memorial Impress'd with the Types of his Own manufacture, and whereas by an Antient Law of this Colony, this Assembly were Graciously Pleased to Enact that any one who should make any Useful Discoveries should Receive an Encouragement there-for from this Honorable Assembly; and as the Manufacture of Types is but in Few hands even in EUROPE, he humbly Conceives it to be a most Valuable Addition to the American Manufacture, and as the Expence of erecting a Proper Foundery will be Great and beyond the abilities of your Memorialist, he humbly hopes for Encouragement from this Assembly Either by Granting him the Liberty of a Lottery for Raising a Sum Sufficient to enable him to carry on the same, or in some other way as to this Honorable Assembly may seem meet; and your Memorialist as in duty Bound shall ever Pray.

Abel Buell

—The University of Virginia Press

Abel Buell made history as the first American type founder. Using his own type here, he petitioned the Connecticut legislature for financial help.

tion, which, by some good Judges in the Printing Way, is allowed to be the neatest ever made in America and equal, if not superior, to any imported from Great-Britain: This Press, we are told, is for Mr. William Goddard, of Philadelphia, Printer.

Several other American colonies beat Connecticut to the making of paper. But in 1766, Christopher Leffingwell established a paper mill at Norwich. A few years later, the Connecticut government fostered his business for a time by paying him a bounty of twopence a quire (24 or 25 sheets) on writing paper and one penny a quire on printing paper.

Paper shortages, however, did plague the newspapers. On August 21, 1775, the *Courant* apologized for appearing on wrapping paper. The printer urged the Daughters of Liberty to save linen and cotton rags for papermaking. A paper mill, he advised, was under construction. A few weeks later, on September 11, the printer was even more apologetic about a two-page edition of his paper:

> ☞ The printer is greatly mortified with the despicable figure of his paper this week, but the Scarcity of the article of paper, and the impossibility of obtaining a supply on any terms, renders it unavoidable. 'Half a loaf, however, is better than no bread.' The news, sometimes, of a half sheet is preferable to that which at other times might be contained in a whole one. As soon as ever paper be had, the *Courant* will recover its usual appearance, and ample amends be made for its present deficiency.

At year's end, the paper mill was still not finished, and the *Courant* actually suspended publication for a month. It then reappeared on inferior paper until March. Thereafter, with its own source of newsprint, the *Courant* started to look better, and the newspaper maintained a standard size of 10 by 16½ inches.

Only once again was the *Courant* to be seriously disturbed in the obtaining of supplies. On January 27, 1778, the paper mill burned down in a fire which some Hartford citizens thought might have been set by Tories. The losses included all of the machinery, 150 reams of writing paper, 100 reams of newsprint, and a quantity of rags and other materials. The Connecticut Assembly came to the newspaper's rescue by authorizing a public lottery of 6,000 tickets at $6 each—$5,000 for a new mill and $31,000 in prizes. In four months, the new mill was producing, and the *Courant* did not miss a single issue thereafter.

Economically, all four newspapers suffered from the inflation that developed during the war. On the eve of the Revolution, the Norwich *Packet* cost 6s. 8d. per year in town and 8s. elsewhere. The *Courant* cost 6s. in Hartford, 8s. by special postrider.

Within a few years, however, the cost of subscriptions rose sharply. The Norwich *Packet* notified readers on May 19, 1777, that its price was going up to 10s. a year, "which is as reasonable as any Paper printed in this or the neighbouring States." Watson of the *Courant* put the matter more feelingly in his edition of May 5, 1777:

> The unreasonable price of the necessaries of life has thrown the Printer into an unhappy dilemma. He must either fling up his business and starve his family, or increase the wages of his workmen, and the price of his News-Paper, and other work. . . . *Twelve shillings* a year, therefore, for the News-Paper, and other work in proportion, is as low as he can possibly afford it, as the times are at present (after which the paper will be cheaper than any of its size on the continent). . . .

On September 10 of the same year, the New Haven *Post Boy* also raised its price to 12s. a year.

And prices continued to rise. The following year, the *Courant* went up to 18s. a year. On October 6, 1778, the same paper announced that payment could be made in the form of "one bushel and three pecks of Wheat, or two bushels and a half of Rye, or three bushels and a half of Indian Corn, or half a hundred of Flour or a Load of Wood or an equivalent in Cash." The following year, the cost of a year's subscription shot to 30s., which "our Customers must judge to be very reasonable, especially considering the great Difficulty, Risque and Expense of procuring Printing Material."

Collecting subscription money was, obviously, a big problem for all the papers, and this very difficulty furnishes us with one of the few solid clues as to the actual circulation of the Hartford *Courant*. Isaiah Thomas, publisher of the Massachusetts *Spy*, said that after the British occupied New York, the circulation of the *Courant* increased rapidly and "for some time, the number of copies printed weekly was equal to, if not greater, than any other paper on the continent."

In 1775, Ebenezer Watson thanked 300 paid-up subscribers and threatened 400 nonpayers with an end to deliveries if they failed to settle—indicating a total circulation of about 700. But in 1778, Hannah Bunce Watson claimed before the state legislature a circulation of 8,000. This figure was very high compared with other American newspapers of the time and with the *Courant* itself after the war, as well as representing a nearly incredible rise in the space of a few years. Authorities differ on how literally one should take Hannah Watson's claim, and no evidence seems decisive. It would seem an extra zero simply crept into Mrs. Watson's report.

Whatever the precise number of subscribers, printers labored to wring payments out of them. Some, like Watson, said that the papers might have to go out of business. He warned, on November 6, 1769, that "by reason of the unexpected and persevering negligence of far the greater part of our customers . . . we are obliged to think of discontinuing the publication of our weekly paper. . . ." Other printers threatened (and perhaps with diminishing effectiveness) to cut off delinquent subscribers. That such threats often failed is clear from a notice in the Norwich *Packet* for October 4, 1781:

> This paper, No. 417, begins the IXth volume of the Norwich Packet. —The Printer having long experienced the perplexities and losses attending outstanding accounts, and the want of punctual payments, earnestly requests all persons whose accounts are of one year's standing, or more, to call and settle them *immediately*. As there are some who have for several years neglected to comply with the repeated requests he has made to them to discharge their respective arrearages, it is presumed they will not wait for any further notice, it being disagreeable to him to put them to cost which he would wish to be unnecessary, or himself to further trouble.—Most kinds of Country Produce, at the current market price, or Connecticut State Money at the common exchange, will be received in payment as readily as Hard Cash.

Timothy Green, publisher of the New London *Gazette,* made an interesting appeal on October 19, 1781, for payment based on his use of type produced by the first American typecaster:

> ∴ The Types on which the Paper is printed (except some Part of the last Page), were manufactured by Mr. Abel Buell, at New-Haven. And as they have been procured by the Printer at great Expense, with a View of serving his Subscribers, as well as himself, he requests such as are indebted to him for News-Papers, etc. would make immediate Payment, that he may be able to comply with his own engagements.

Postriders, who delivered the newspapers out of town, were responsible for collecting from the more distant subscribers. A favorite path for the intercolonial, and later interstate riders, was the Boston Post Road, leaving New Haven and reaching Boston by three alternative routes passing through Connecticut, Rhode Island, and Massachusetts. At each stop, the postrider would sound his trumpet to alert subscribers and others of his arrival. He blew his trumpet once again half an hour before leaving town.

The routes of a local New Haven *Post Boy* rider may be seen from a notice Nathan Hicok, Jr., inserted on October 18, 1781, for the collection of debts. He was to be in Washington on Monday the 19th, East Greenwich on Tuesday, and Kent on Wednesday. The following month he planned to be in Woodbury on Monday, November 5th; Southbury on Tuesday; Wednesday in Oxford; Thursday at Henry Tomlinson's in Derby; and Friday at Isaac Smith's in Derby. At each of these places he stood ready to accept subscription money at one o'clock in the afternoon. Mr. Hicok also apprised the public he would be selling writing paper, Dillworth's Spelling Book, and primers at his stops.

War News, Far and Near

WAR news dominated Connecticut newspapers during the Revolution and colored much else that appeared in them. Usually such news was aimed at raising the spirits of readers or inflaming their feelings against the British. American victories were emphasized, while British victories were discounted or explained away. Thus, the *Courant* portrayed William Howe's occupation of Philadelphia in 1777 as a triumph for General Washington. According to this account, Washington had escaped a trap and lured Howe into a position from which he could not retreat safely. In fact, the British troops relaxed in the captured city for the winter, while the Americans were going through the agony of Valley Forge.

The realities of the war, however, could be judged by ads such as the one in the *Courant* for April 7, 1777, for nurses and hospital supplies. "Steady Women" were offered $1 a week to work in United States Army hospitals. The steward of the American Hospital also called for large quantities of "Baum, Oatmeal, Tammarines, old Linnen, Rags or Lint, Beeswax and Oyl."

But Connecticut newspapers offered inspiration, too, for the Patriot cause. On April 28, 1777, the Norwich *Packet* gave an account of the death of a Lieutenant Gregory, whose last words echoed those of Nathan Hale the previous year. Carried wounded off the field, he called his men to him and said as he lay dying:

> Countrymen and fellow-soldiers, I shall leave you in a few minutes. All that I am sorry for is, that I did not live longer to be of service to my bleeding country. Be brave, my lads, and acquit yourself like men! Maintain your own liberty, and that of your country!

The British army was sometimes ridiculed by the Connecticut newspapers as incompetent—but more often vituperated as cruel and bloody. Hessians were especially feared. A writer in the Norwich *Packet* for July 1, 1776, predicted hysterically that the cruelty of the German mercenaries would "make the ears of our posterity, the millions who are yet unborn, tingle, when they read the transaction in the pages of some future history."

On January 1, 1777, a broadside poem published in Norwich purported to speak for the Howe brothers—General William and Admiral Richard Howe. The following stanzas convey the broadside's tone:

> Asking no questions, you must instantly take,
> Such laws as are made, or our Masters shall make;
> We claim all your Persons and all your Estates,
> To serve our *King George*, and to pay all his Rates.

You see the good *Tories,* consent all about,
Blame none of our laws, abett none of your rout;
They give us their children, their wives & their wealth,
We hold, all that do not, are guilty of stealth.

The atrocity stories carried more sting. In the Norwich *Packet* for May 19, 1777, William Gamble, apparently a freed American prisoner of the British, described the horrors of life on a prison ship. Inmates, he said, were not allowed the use of a swab or broom to keep the main deck, and thus themselves, dry. Meat, served from a pickle cask at nine in the morning, had to be cooked soon because the fire was put out at around noon. Prisoners had neither butter nor cheese and only bad oil. They received only one gill of weak rum a day. Worst of all, the men were sometimes kept for as long as 12 or 16 hours a day without a drop of water.

Even more distressing for newspaper readers were reports such as one relayed by William Gordon of Roxbury to the New Haven *Post Boy* of April 16, 1777. The writer of the report, from Newark, New Jersey, described the alleged assaults of British marauders in his section of the country. He told of widespread rape, one victim being a woman 70 years old. Despite a promise that townspeople who stayed in their homes would not be molested, soldiers sacked and then burned many homes. Old people and the ill were hauled out of bed and terrorized. Even officers allegedly took part in these outrages. And Tory leanings turned out to be of no help. One ardent Tory met the British troops in the street with cheers. But his house was reportedly looted, his shoes stolen off his feet, and his life threatened.

The effect of such items on an already excited public can readily be imagined. The dominant part of the Connecticut public already looked on British troops as oppressors. No one knew where the enemy might strike next, and newspapers kept giving accounts of soldiers running wild in conquered towns. One-sided reporting that magnified and dwelt upon enemy atrocities helped sustain Connecticut's zeal for the Revolution.

Connecticut towns along the coast, within easy reach of the British in New York, had good reason indeed to fear attack. A few score troops were early stationed at New London, New Haven, Lyme, and Stonington to forestall such a possibility. The British, however, did not strike until April, 1777, and then they moved inland quickly to a target some distance from the coast.

On April 25, Major General William Tryon, royal governor of New York, landed at Cedar Point, east of Norwalk. His goal was the Patriot supply depot in Danbury some 20 miles away. In an exceptionally factual manner, the New Haven *Post Boy* for April 30, 1777, described the enemy advance, the occupation of the town, the destruction of supplies, and the firing of Patriot property.

46

General Benedict Arnold, who happened to be visiting his sister in Connecticut at the time, led several hundred men in harassment of the withdrawing British forces. The *Post Boy's* account of Arnold's conduct at Ridgefield captures the man's intrepidity:

> . . . the General had his horse shot under him, when the enemy were within about ten yards of him, but luckily received no hurt, recovering himself he drew his pistols and shot the soldier who was advancing with his fixed bayonet.—He then ordered his troops to retreat thro' a shower of small, and grape shot. In this action the enemy suffered very considerably, leaving about thirty dead and wounded on the ground, besides a number unknown, buried.

The *Post Boy's* account of these matters was delivered in terse style, understating British losses at "more than double our number." In fact, the British losses were more than *treble* the American. Only near the end of its report did the newspaper give way to indignation:

> The enemy on this occasion behaved with their usual barbarity, wantonly and cruelly murdering the wounded prisoners who fell into their hands, and plundering the inhabitants, burning and destroying everything in their way.

Once again, Connecticut Tories suffered the consequences of British aggression, and the *Post Boy* concluded: "Since the enemy went off, a number of disaffected Persons, who it is supposed intended to join them, have been taken into Custody."

Two years later, a series of attacks along the coast once again brought the violence of war home to Connecticut citizens. On July 5, 1779, Major General Tryon, this time leading 2,600 troops, descended upon West Haven. Only limited destruction took place, for the principal goal of the British was to intimidate Connecticut Patriots. However, the *Post Boy* for July 7, 1779, angrily cited a number of atrocities, including "the beating, stabbing and insulting of the Rev. Dr. Daggett after he was made a prisoner." What the newspaper failed to point out was that the elderly Naphtali Daggett, President *Emeritus* of Yale College, had been sniping with a long fowling rifle at the British. After capture, the old man would not promise to stop harassing the invaders and finally exhausted their patience.

Before returning to New York, Tryon landed at Fairfield and almost completely destroyed the town by fire—the worst of his actions in this campaign. The New London *Gazette* for August 4, 1779, gave a searing account of Hessian brutality:

> The parties that were first set loose for rapine and plunder, were the Hessians.—They entered the houses, attacked the persons of Whig and Tory indiscriminately, breaking open desks, trunks, closets, chests, and taking away everything of value; they robbed women of buckles, rings, bonnets, aprons and handkerchiefs; they abused them with the foulest

—*The Hartford Courant*

This man inks type on what is believed to be the *Courant*'s original printing press. In colonial times he would not have worn finery for such work.

and most profane language, threatened their lives, presenting bayonets to their breasts, not in the least regarding the most earnest cries and intreaties; there was likewise heard the dashing of looking glasses, furniture, china, and whatever came in their power.

With a shrewd eye to its effect on Patriot ardor, the July 7, 1779, New Haven *Post Boy* quoted a flyer that the British had left in the towns attacked. This pointed out the vulnerability of Connecticut to British retaliation:

> Your towns, your property, yourselves, lie within the grasp of the power whose forbearance, you have ungenerously construed into fear; but whose lenity has persisted in its mild & noble efforts, even tho' branded with the most unworthy imputation.
>
> The existence of a single habitation on your defenceless coast, ought to be a constant reproof to your ingratitude. Can the strength of your whole province cope with the force which might at any time be poured through every district in your country? . . . You who lie so much in our power, afford that most striking monument of our mercy, and therefore ought to set the first example of returning to allegiance. . . .

General Tryon apparently thought that Connecticut Patriots could be cowed, but the publication of his arrogance could only have steeled the will of the revolutionaries. Nevertheless, the raids made the people of Connecticut more apprehensive. The *Post Boy* for August 4, 1779, noted the alarm in New London at "38 sail of shipping coming down the Sound." In that case, the fear was groundless.

Yet New London's time was to come, with the worst of the British land-sea assaults on Connecticut. On September 6, 1781, a fleet of 32 British ships carrying 1,700 troops arrived in New London Harbor. The leader was none other than General Benedict Arnold, a native of Norwich and back in 1777 a brave defender of his state, but now employed by the British. After a sharp battle, Fort Griswold fell to the attackers, who lost about forty killed and one-hundred wounded. In one of the most shameful incidents of the entire war, the British evened scores by butchering some eighty Americans *after* they had surrendered. Not only did the British destroy American shipping in the harbor, they also set fires in town that ran out of control and turned New London into a smoldering ruin.

There was no need for Connecticut papers to embroider the slaughter in New London, and the bloodshed was made all the more intolerable by the role in it of the state's and country's archtraitor. Without comment, the New Haven *Post Boy* for September 27, 1781, published General Howe's praise for the traitor Arnold's "precaution to prevent the destruction of the Town, which is a misfortune that gives him much Concern." The following week, the *Post Boy's* front page was taken up with Arnold's cold-blooded description to Howe of the New London raid, an account omitting the numerous atrocities that made the event hideous. Once again, the newspaper's lack of editorial comment spoke far more eloquently to Connecticut readers than partisan language.

Anger at Arnold ran especially deep in Connecticut, however, and the entire front page of the Hartford *Courant* for October 23, 1781, was given over to "The Life and CHARACTER of General ARNOLD, extracted from the new History of the American Revolution." There, readers were informed:

> Gold was the lodestone of his heart. He did not deliberate a moment whether he should accept the bribe. He was of no country—of no party —and of no religion—and therefore he had no objection to closing with Sir Henry's [Sir Henry Clinton's] bargain.

Privateers had done much to arouse Britsh concern about Connecticut shore towns. These free-lance members of the American naval forces struck some telling blows against British shipping. Advertisements, especially in the New London *Gazette*, sought sailors "desirous of serving their Country and adding to their Fortunes" (*Gazette* for October 12, 1781) and also gave news of the sale of prize goods.

And sometimes the sea yielded eerie mementoes of the war. The following item from the issue of the New London *Gazette* cited above conveys all the terror of a Scottish ballad:

> Thursday of last week, an officer, sewed in a hammock, was found drove ashore on the southside of Fisher's Island: he had on a superfine red broadcloth coat, and was otherwise well-dressed.

Life on the Home Front

THE fortunes of war made a considerable impact on Connecticut's cultural life, as many news items testify. For example, the British raid on New Haven in the summer of 1779 led to cancellation of the Yale commencement, scheduled for September. President Ezra Stiles gave notice of the cancellation in the New Haven *Post Boy* of August 11, 1779. But he called on candidates for "the *first* and *second* Degrees" to come to New Haven on Wednesday, September 8 to receive their diplomas. Those seeking admission to the college were also invited to take their entrance examinations at the same time. Although the town of New Haven was regarded as being in too dangerous a situation for all the undergraduates to return to classes, President Stiles wanted the students to continue their studies at home "until God in his Providence may permit them to be peaceably re-assembled at this Seat of Learning."

Economically, Yale was feeling the pinch of inflation, and the *Post Boy* for October 13, 1779, carried an ad soliciting provisions for the college:

> The Steward of Yale College wants to purchase Wheat or Wheat Flour, Pork and Beef, Butter and Cheese, for which he will give a good Price. He desires those Parents and Guardians who have Children at College, to afford him what Assistance in this Way they can. The Steward has good Rock Salt to exchange for Butter.

By the middle of the Revolution, the economic disruption of Connecticut was widespread, and newspapers and broadsides bore ample evidence of distress. A broadside published April 1, 1778, in New London set forth price controls for the county of that name—a policy being tried out by other Connecticut counties as well.

From it we can learn the standard *day's* wages in that county of various occupations: A common laborer earned, along with two meals, 4*s*. 6*d*. in the summer; 3*s*. 6*d*. in the spring and fall; and 2*s*. 6*d*. in the winter. A male tailor earned 4*s*. 6*d*.—but a woman only half as much!

Times got worse toward the end of the war. The Hartford *Courant* described an attempt to ease the poverty of a minister and his family:

> East Hartford, April 3, 1783
> Yesterday a number of Young Ladies, and others, as a testimony of their respect and kindness to their Minister and his Family, generously presented to his Lady, upwards of an hundred [word uncertain] of Linen Yarn, and divers other valuable articles; which was very thankfully accepted. An example worthy of imitation, especially at the present day, amidst the difficulties that have arisen from our distressing times, which have been sorely felt by many people, but have fallen with peculiar weight upon Ministers and their families, depriving in many instances, of the means of subsistance, as well as decencies of life.

Yet business went on, and some of the ads for merchandise have a naive tone refreshing in an era when depth psychology has found a home on Madison Avenue. The following appeared in the *Courant* for March 20, 1775:

> WHALE BONE, and Black SEWING SILK,
> TO BE SOLD BY
> William Beadle,
> In Queen-Street, WETHERSFIELD,
> WITH
>
> 4*d*. Nails, and 6*d*. Nails, and 8*d*. Nails, and 10*d*. Nails, and 12*d*. Nails, and 20*d*. Nails; and some that look large enough to be Grand-Fathers to any of the other sorts. Also about half a Dozen other Articles for Sale, at the same Place.

☞ I wonder whether this Advertisement will do any GOOD? ☜

Early Americans got plenty of mileage out of publications. Reading aloud was an act of frugality that kept nonreaders informed while saving money.

Just over a month later, Beadle was back with an advertisement headed "GUN POWDER." This time he offered:

2 or 3 Hundred other Articles, which I Sell so Cheap that I cannot afford to Pay the Printer for telling you their Names; therefore would be glad if you would please to come & Buy them without my Advertising them at large.

Beadle apparently became the subject of an advertisement himself in the New Haven *Post Boy* for April 10, 1783. The Reverend James Dana of Wallingford offered, at the price of one shilling each, printed copies of his sermon called *MEN'S sins not chargeable on God, but on themselves*. It dealt with William Beadle's murder of his wife and four children in Wethersfield, followed by his suicide.

The effectiveness of word-of-mouth solicitation in the small communities of Revolutionary Connecticut and the absence of large-scale industry made Help Wanted advertisements uncommon. Yet some of the exceptions are especially interesting in view of the war, such as the following in the New London *Gazette* for September 28, 1781:

The SHIP
F O R T U N E
Commanded by HENRY BILLINGS.
Being compleatly fitted as a Privateer, and equiped with 16 nine-pound Cannon, will sail on a Cruize on or before the last of this Month:
All Gentlemen Seamen or Landsmen who are desirous of adding to their Fortunes, will meet suitable Encouragement by a timely Application on Board.
New-London, 21st Sept. 1781

Throughout the economic and military turmoil, Connecticut retained its prewar love of learning. Print shops offered grammars, works in Greek and Latin, studies in mathematics and philosophy, and political tracts. Schools, too, never ceased to run advertisements in the newspapers for pupils. The breadth of some of their curricula may be gauged from the following ad, placed in the *Courant* for April 17, 1775:

Taught in the Grammar School at *Hartford*, the Greek and Latin Languages, for the Purpose of preparing youth for the College.—Those who can tarry long enough at the School, and request it, may in the Course of their Education, be instructed in Writing, Arithmetic, and the Art of Speaking; also Geography, by a new and easy Method, the Elements of Geometry, Trigonometry, the Art of Navigation, Surveying, &c. A Watchful Eye is kept over the Morals of the Youth; and unwearied attempts made to enrich their Minds with virtuous Sentiments, and the Principles of the Christian Religion. . . .

Numerous other schools—typically located in the schoolmaster's house—announced themselves to the world through newspapers. Not all tried to cover the full range of a liberal education, and some specialized in business subjects or music, for example. On June 5, 1781, however, Noah Webster, Jr., advertised through the *Courant* a school in Sharon with a curriculum as broad as that outlined above. Webster, destined for greater fame as the author of spellers and dictionaries, stated that tuition would cost "the moderate price of Six Dollars and two thirds per quarter per scholar."

And Connecticut newspapers showed the same lively interest in natural phenomena—earthquakes, lightning, and such—during the war as before. In 1769, the *Courant* reported the appearance of a comet over Connecticut and then followed the report with a series of essays seeking to explain comets. In 1780, the occurrence of an eclipse of the sun prompted the *Courant* to ask its readers to send in the times of its appearance and disappearance, the color of nearby clouds, and other data.

Some of these reports of the marvelous amounted to little dramas, and the following account in the New Haven *Post Boy* for August 4, 1779, described the adventure of three men in New London Harbor:

> Last Friday, three of the militia, belonging to Capt. Raynsford's company from Canterbury, viz. William Baldwin, John Bayer, and Jeremiah Mott, having been fishing near the light-house, at the mouth of this harbour, in a small canoe, on their return to shore, in about four feet water, they discovered a large shark, (which afterwards proved to be 9 and a half feet long) making towards them, with great fury, and struck the canoe with such force as to throw Mott into the water: The other two seeing their companion in danger of being devoured, leaped into the water, and one of them seized the shark by the tail, while the other played the paddle so effectually to his head, that after a considerable struggle they killed it, and afterwards brought it to town. The curiosity drew together a great number of spectators.

Winding Down of Hostilities

Nᴇᴡs of the climactic surrender of Lord Charles Cornwallis at Yorktown, Virginia, on October 19, 1781, filtered back slowly to Connecticut. On October 30, the *Courant* carried a brief report of the event, conveyed by schooner from the scene. On November 1, the Norwich *Packet* ran a letter from a man in New Haven to a friend in Norwich regarding plans for a victory celebration in New Haven:

Joy reigns unbounded—hope gleams from every countenance—providence favours us—America prospers—and Liberty smiles. We heard of the capture yesterday morning; bells and cannon welcomed the news with sounds more agreeable than usual. The town will be illuminated tomorrow evening, and next day an elegant entertainment at the court-house, accompanied with all the military parade usual on such occasions. O we feel the glorious event in every nerve!

The New Haven *Post Boy* for November 8 concisely described the celebration itself:

In this town, on Monday last, a numerous assembly convened at the Brick Meeting-House, where the audience were highly entertained, with an animating, pathetic and ingenious Oration, delivered by one of the Tutors of the College, and a triumphant hymn sung by the Students;—the clergy and a number of other gentlemen dined in the State-House;—in the evening the State-House, College, and all the Houses round the Market-Place, were beautifully illuminated:—The Whole was conducted with the greatest regularity, good-nature, festivity and joy.

At last, almost a month after Yorktown, the *Courant* led off its issue for November 13 with letters and documents from George Washington and Lord Cornwallis regarding the British surrender. The details must have come as an anticlimax, but the public obviously could not hear too much of the joyous news. The following week, the *Courant* gloated over the discomfiture of the Loyalist newspapers in New York:

All the late New-York papers have at length confessed the surrender of Lord Cornwallis to be real. They have even condescended to insert the articles of capitulation verbatim from the Philadelphia gazettes. The women are in tears, the soldiery in a panic, the merchants selling off their goods for much less than the first cost in Europe, the tories are in the utmost consternation, and Benedict Arnold himself, it is said trembles like an aspen leaf—in the midst of this scene of distress and wretchedness, with a superior French fleet on the coast ready to swallow them, the demagogues of that city are publishing in their gazettes contents of rebel mails and criticisms upon poems written by the King of Prussia; which conduct is full as ridiculous and stupid as if a criminal on his way to the gallows, and sitting on his coffin, should at the same time be amusing himself with Ben Johnson's jests, or writing strictures on the stile and language of the sheriff's warrant which condemns him to be hanged.

Connecticut newspapers were no more generous to the defeated general than they were to the Loyalist newspapers. The Norwich *Packet* for November 29 picked up from the Pennsylvania *Journal* an imaginary account of Cornwallis' reception as he rode through the parts of Virginia he had ravaged. The fictional citizens said:

1. You murdered my father in cold blood. 2. You starved my husband. 3. You hung my son. 4. You bayoneted my brother after he surrendered. 5. You burnt my house. 6. You burnt my barn. 7. You stole my grain. 8. You stole my negroes. 9. You stole my English horse. . . .

And so on for a total of 31 accusations.

Yet the article urged readers not to be too hasty in punishing Cornwallis. According to the fantasy, George Washington shook his hand and sent him an invitation to dinner—upon which:

> His Lordship, knowing his deserts, was overcome by his magnanimity. It was not till then he felt the utmost exacerbation of human misery. He became frantic with grief. He wrung his hands, and threw himself upon his mattress. His whole frame was agitated, and nature sunk into a fever, which prevented his Lordship from accepting of his Excellency's invitation. He read the card over and over.—"It is impossible!—no 'tis his Excellency's hand writing! O godlike generosity!—I now feel for the *first time,* compunction for the ravages I have committed upon this country. . . ."

In conclusion of the fantasy, George Washington allowed the repentant Cornwallis to return to England and public shame.

Despite the victory at Yorktown, the war still dragged on in the countryside, and Tories and Indians continued to raid outlying settlements. The United States—and Connecticut—had to remain in a state of preparedness. Connecticut newspapers reflected the strain of waiting for a definite end to hostilities. For example, the New London *Gazette* for April 25, 1783, carried still another atrocity report in a letter signed "An American." The author charged that 1,644 Americans died on the British prison ship *Jersey* moored off New York—because of "inhumane, cruel, and savage and barbarous usage." He warned the British to "tremble lest the vengeance of Heaven fall on your Isle, for the blood of these unfortunate victims!"

The New Haven *Post Boy* for April 17, 1783, carried news that the war was at last effectively concluded with the preliminary Treaty of Paris. The ship *Astrea* had brought the news from France to Salem, Massachusetts, in the unusually fast time of 22 days. Yet many embittered Americans could not bring themselves to forgive the Tories in their midst. The same issue of the *Post Boy* printed on its front page the minutes of a town meeting in Stratford dealing with the question of Tories wishing to return. The report began:

> While we rejoice at the opening prospects for Peace, we feel ourselves exceedingly alarmed, to see whole shoals of Tories, and Disaffected Persons, flocking over from Long-Island, and other parts within the enemy's lines, in order to take refuge among the virtuous friends of our country; altho' the King of Great-Britain has made provision for such kind of persons, to take up their residence in the province of Nova Scotia.—Whereupon this Meeting came into the following Resolves:

FIRST, That we will not countenance, or give our consent, that any person, or persons, of the above description, shall be admitted, or suffered to reside in this town, until the Public Authority of this State, shall have decided upon the matter; but, on the contrary, we do pledge our honor, to each other, that we will exert ourselves, in the most proper and strenuous manner, to drive off and expel all such persons who shall make the attempt to regain that settlement in this town, which they have utterly and forever forfeited.

The resolutions following dealt with specific Tories trying to return to Stratford. One Edward DeForest attracted special opprobrium. He had joined the British five or six years previous, actually taking some townspeople as prisoners. He had recently come back to town, "publicly to walk the streets of Freedom." The meeting ordered him seized, sent to Fairfield, and then consigned to the British. William Hurd and Abel Fairchild, who had joined the British several years before, defended themselves unsuccessfully before the meeting and were ordered sent back to the British. Anthony Baker, who did not appear, suffered the same fate.

It is pleasant to report that most Connecticut Loyalists received kinder treatment. Rehabilitation of defeated enemies was the more common policy of the Patriots.

Veterans of the Continental Army, meanwhile, clamored for a settlement by Congress of their claims for pay and supplies. The entire front page of the New Haven *Post Boy* for April 24, 1783, was occupied by resolutions and a statement by what was described as a meeting of the Federal Army in New Windsor. An address to army officers called upon them to become more militant in their demands lest they be "the only sufferers by this revolution" and "grow old in poverty, wretchedness, and contempt."

The *Post Boy* for May 1, nevertheless, described widespread public rejoicing in town, followed by a startling toast:

> Accordingly, the day with the rising sun, was ushered in, by the discharge of Thirteen Cannon, paraded on the green for that purpose, under elegant silk colours, with the Coat of Arms of the United States most ingeniously represented thereon, which was generously contributed upon the occasion by the ladies of the town.
>
> At 9 o'clock in the forenoon, the inhabitants met in the brick Meeting-House for divine service, where were convened a very crowded Assembly: The service was opened with an anthem: Then a very pertinent prayer, together with thanksgiving, was made by the Rev. Dr. Stiles, President of Yale-College; after was sung some lines purposely composed for the occasion, by the singers of all the congregations, in consort: Then followed a very ingenious Oration, spoken by Mr. Elizur Goodrich, one of the Tutors of the College; after which a very liberal collection was made for the poor of the town, to elevate their hearts for rejoicing. The service concluded with an anthem.

MONDAY MARCH 19, 1770.

THE

Connecticut COURANT.

Containing the freshest Advices Both Foreign and Domestic

N*umb* 273.

MONDAY, February 19, 1776.   THE   NUMBER 578

CONNECTICUT   COURANT

A N D   HARTFORD

WEEKLY   INTELLIGENCER

Containing the Freshest ADVICES,   Both FOREIGN and DOMESTIC.

PRINTED AND PUBLISHED BY *EBENEZER WATSON*, NEAR THE GREAT BRIDGE.

The Connecticut Courant AND
WEEKLY INTELLIGENCER.
TUESDAY, November 19, 1781.   (No. 877)
HARTFORD: Printed by HUDSON AND GOODWIN, NEAR THE GREAT BRIDGE.

Courant masthead reflected Connecticut politics. Royal emblem gave way in Revolution to state's trio of grapevines, then to republican simplicity.

A number of the most respectable gentlemen of the town dined together at the Coffee-House: After dinner the following toasts were drank;

1. United States of America.
2. Congress.
3. His Most Christian Majesty.
4. The United Provinces.

During the following weeks, Connecticut newspapers continued to record the distress of the British government over its defeat. The *Post Boy* for May 8, 1783, offered long excerpts from a speech to the House of Commons by William Pitt the Younger, asserting that the war "cost 5 million more than all the wars of the last age, including the splendid and important victories of the Duke of Marlborough."

Continuing to rub in the British defeat, the *Post Boy* in the same month picked up a column of quotations from the London *Daily Courant* for January 3, 1783:

"This kingdom is sovereign and supreme over America, and taxation is part of that power. Tell me when the Americans were emancipated."

G. Grenville.

"To maintain the authority of this kingdom, I would enforce a tax from America, though it were but a pepper corn."

Nugent.

"They shall put their necks under our feet."

North.

"I shall move that courts of vice-admiralty have further powers, and that offenders in America be brought from thence to England for trial; and that three-pence per pound duty be imposed on tea, payable in Boston and other parts of the colonies."

Late Charles Townshend.

And nine more quotations followed, until the concluding paragraph: "Such are the extracts of speeches, by which this country has lost America FOR EVER."

The New Haven *Post Boy* for May 22, 1783, looked forward as well as backward. On the front page it carried the following token of budding nationalism:

These are to notify the Members of the First Medical Society in the Thirteen United States of America, since their Independence, that a Meeting will be holden at the House of Doct. Phineas Smith, in Sharon, on the Second Tuesday of June next, at Ten o'Clock A.M.

In the next column appeared an uncharacteristic item—a letter from a British officer who viewed the evacuation of Charlestown. He described the orderly transfer of authority from British to American hands. Many Loyalists, he said, chose to remain behind, but most preferred to abandon their belongings and depart with their British protectors. He pulled out all the stops in describing the departing Loyalists as they left their friends:

> As these pass'd the windows of their friends and acquaintances, in their way to the places of embarkation, they silently, with grief unutterable, bowed their last farewell. This melancholy salute was returned with feelings that could only be expressed by tears and sobs. A gloomy despair sat on every countenance; and all was wretchedness and woe.
>
> The scene was too affecting for description, too great for human feelings. Even the most obdurate and unprincipled of your Patriots, had he been present at this awful view; must have felt some remorse for the part he has acted, and lamented the falsities he has palmed on Parliament as facts, and which have brought the most complicated misery and ruin on thousands and thousands, whose only crime has been loyalty to their King, and affection for their parent country.

Legacy

WITH the Revolution's fulfillment, the zeal of the Connecticut press died down. The success of their cause had to have a calming effect on the editor-printers. And nearly 20 years of strident advocacy (since the Stamp Act) must have wearied editors and readers alike.

The New London *Gazette* traded its defiance of British authority for loyalty to the Federalist administrations of Washington and John Adams. Even more striking was the posture of the Hartford *Courant*. After heartily supporting the Federal Constitution in 1787, it condemned democracy as mob rule a few years later. Jarvis Means Morse in his Tercentenary Commission *Pamphlet* on the Connecticut press observes: "Until about 1800, [the editor] generally suppressed partisan communications, and instead filled the *Courant* pages with literary productions—the poems of the Hartford Wits, lectures on modern history, and lengthy extracts from the British *Annual Register*."

Yet the Revolutionary (and revolutionary) performance of Connecticut printers, along with that of their counterparts in other states, invigorated freedom of the press in America. Editors and reporters in the United States have never completely forgotten that early printers defied authority over the Stamp Act, mobilized public opinion, and finally hastened the triumph of a bold new idea over hallowed tradition.

To this day, however, the challenge raised by the Revolutionary press—paced by the printers in Hartford, New Haven, New London, and Norwich—remains unanswered: How far does freedom of the American press extend? In fact, are there any limits at all? The political events of the 1970s, with the press as sounding board, certainly have not resolved such questions. The printer-editors of Connecticut, like many Patriot leaders, reached deeper into the future than they ever thought.

For Further Reading

The newspapers cited in the text were the main source used in the preparation of this booklet.

Bailyn, Bernard. *The Ideological Origins of the American Revolution*. Cambridge: Harvard University Press, 1967.

Bates, Albert C. *Thomas Green*. New Haven: New Haven Historical Society Papers, Vol. VIII, 1914.

Brigham, Clarence S. *History and Bibliography of American Newspapers, 1690-1820*. Worcester, Mass.: American Antiquarian Society, 1947.

————. *Journals and Journeymen*. Philadelphia: University of Pennsylvania Press, 1950.

Davidson, Philip. *Propaganda and the American Revolution*. Chapel Hill: The University of North Carolina Press, 1941.

McNulty, John Bard. *Older Than the Nation*. Chester, Conn.: Pequot Press, 1964.

Morse, Jarvis Means. *Connecticut Newspapers in the Eighteenth Century*. New Haven: Yale University Press, 1935.

Royster, Vermont. *The American Press and the Revolutionary Tradition*. Washington: American Enterprise Institute for Public Policy Research, 1974.

Schlesinger, Arthur M. *Prelude to Independence*. New York: Knopf, 1958.

Silver, Rollo G. *The American Printer 1787-1825*. Charlottesville: The University of Virginia Press, 1967.

Smith, J. Eugene. *One Hundred Years of Hartford's Courant*. New Haven: Yale University Press, 1949.

White, Herbert H. *British Prisoners-of-War in Hartford During the Revolution*. New Haven: New Haven Historical Society *Papers*, Vol. VIII, 1914.